WOMEN PROPHETS OF THE OLD TESTAMENT

KIERAN LARKIN

Copyright © 2022 by Kieran Larkin

Published by Red Penguin Books

All rights reserved.
No part of this book may be reproduced in any form or by any electronic or mechanical means, including information storage and retrieval systems, without written permission from the author, except for the use of brief quotations in a book review.

CONTENTS

Preface	v
1. The Role of Women in Ancient Israel and Judah	1
2. What Makes a Prophetess "Prophetic?"	17

ACKNOWLEDGED PROPHETS

3. Sarah	25
4. Miriam	37
5. Deborah	49
6. Hannah	63
7. Abigail	75
8. "The Prophetess"	87
9. Huldah	95
10. Noadiah	115
11. Esther	123

PROPHETS "ON THE BUBBLE"

12. Rebekah	143
13. Rahab	161
14. Samson's Mother, the Wife of Manoah	173
15. Queen Mother of Lemuel	179
16. The Female Guild Prophets	187
Epilogue	193
Bibliography	195
About the Author	199
Also by Kieran Larkin	201

PREFACE

Many years ago, when I attended Catholic parochial school in Brooklyn, New York, the boys and girls were separated into different divisions when we reached the fifth grade—and we remained separated until graduation. When I began my high school career, I attended an all-boys Catholic secondary school for another four years prior to entering college. In other words, I was essentially "quarantined" from girls from the age of ten to the age of eighteen. And while my college—like most colleges these days—was coeducational, I have spent the last 37 years of my life teaching in a prestigious all-girls Catholic high school. So I am very familiar with two important things: the advantages and disadvantages of single-sex education and the unequal treatment of women in today's world in society, in government and in the Church. And this inequality has gnawed away at my psyche and moral compass to a point where it both angers and frustrates me. As a grown man who finds himself surrounded by intelligent, resourceful and dynamic young women each and every day, I find it impossible to adequately address their questions, concerns and frustrations when such inequality becomes the topic du jour.

Last year I wrote a book entitled *Messengers of God: A Survey of Old Testament Prophets*. My goals in writing this book were threefold: first, to discover if I had the stamina to write an entire book (much to my surprise, it turned out that I did!); second, to research and to present material about a group of Old Testament heroes I truly admired; and third, to compose a textbook I hoped to use in a course on the Prophetic Books of the Old Testament that I was offering to my senior class students. As you can probably imagine, this largest part of this book featured many of the popular prophets whose names are recognized even by those with no real interest in either Scripture or spiritual studies—prophets such as Isaiah, Jeremiah, Ezekiel, Daniel, Elijah and a host of others.

When I proudly announced to my classes that I had written a book—and proceeded to outline its contents—one of my students promptly raised her hand and asked, "Are there any women prophets in your book?" It was at that moment that I realized I had "missed the boat" in a profound way. Here I was, priding myself on my feminist philosophy, thinking I was not only incredibly broadminded but genuinely sensitive to issues of importance to women, and I had failed miserably to address a key issue of significance to the young women I purport to serve. At least this innocent "wakeup call" didn't fall on deaf ears! And, as a result, this book began to take form—a presentation of women prophets of the Old Testament whose call to serve as messengers of God played as much of a pivotal role in salvation history and in the development of the Chosen People as the ministries and preachings of the male prophets.

At the risk of appearing to make excuses, I would like to point out—with some degree of accuracy, I think—that far fewer women prophets are featured in the Old Testament than male prophets. Additionally, there also seems to be much less written material in Scripture to "flesh out" their ministries. Nevertheless and notwithstanding, it is my hope and wish to present them as the heroes (or is that heroines?) they are—women hand-picked by God to complete vital work, women worthy of respect, admiration and emulation for their obvious dedication and passion to complete the work entrusted to them by God. It is entirely possible that the number of women prophets is far greater than we realize. Very possibly their words and ministries were deemed (chauvinistically) to be unworthy of inclusion in Sacred Scripture and have been lost in the mists of history. We may never know if this theory is well-founded unless it is brought to light by some future archaeological discoveries. In the meantime, however, we can "accentuate the positive" and focus renewed attention on the women prophets we *do* know.

Throughout this book I have chosen to present Scriptural passages from the *Good News Bible: Today's English Version,* published in 1976 by the American Bible Society (Imprimatur: Archbishop John Francis Whealon of Hartford, Connecticut). I find this translation of the Old Testament to be eminently readable and mellifluous. It's the translation I use in class with my students.

Throughout my life I have been blessed by the presence of many, many accomplished, vibrant, passionate and deeply spiritual women who have helped to shape me and guide me on the paths I travel. My mother may be the most prayerful and faith-filled woman I have ever met, and my two sisters, Eileen and Janet, are the proverbial "apples that don't fall far from the tree." My wife Stephanie is a rare combination of Ann Landers and Indian Point—possessing the sensitivity of spirit displayed by the advice columnist and the endless energy generated by a nuclear power plant. And, like Don Quixote, she never views any of her dreams as impossible. Similarly, my daughter Kathleen and my niece Alison display a depth of passion and a commitment to authentic human values that is personally inspirational, and my mother-in-law Chris possesses an artistic vision and an indomitable spirit—a latter-day Rosie the Riveter. The women who are my academic colleagues are either Sisters of St. Joseph (of Brentwood, New York) or lay teachers, both married and single, but they collectively present themselves to our students not only as accomplished academic professionals, but as paradigms of faith and role models. And finally, my students grow from girls into young women and from confused and awkward youngsters into confident, mature and committed adults before my eyes. Yes, I have been blessed by the presence of incredible women throughout my whole life—and I dedicate this book to each and every one of them.

Chapter One

THE ROLE OF WOMEN IN ANCIENT ISRAEL AND JUDAH

When Jesus began His public ministry at approximately the age of thirty, His impact on the people of Judah (Judea) was profound. His many sermons—be they in a temple or on a hillside or from a boat moored in one of the lakes of Judea—excited and challenged His listeners. His words spoke of a loving God whose compassion for His people was boundless, but He also condemned injustice, judgmentalism and hypocrisy, rankling and infuriating the Judean religious leaders who were often His target. In addition to His preaching, the miracles Jesus performed altered the landscape of Judean life in ways that were both profound and controversial. Curing people with physical handicaps, casting out "demons" (more probably curing victims of epilepsy or psychological/emotional difficulties), and raising the dead not only placed Jesus "center stage" but taught the Judeans how they must reach out to help one another. *Love one another as I have loved you...* (John 13:34)

Lost to many among these extraordinary signs and wonders was the revolutionary way that Jesus approached and related to women. Whether it was His sensitivity to the woman with profound monthly bleeding (Luke 8:43-48) or His mercy to the woman caught in adultery (John 8:3-11), it was remarkably counter-cultural for Jesus to treat the women of His day with such deference and respect. Therefore, it was no wonder that a number of women, such as Mary Magdalene, Joanna and Susanna, chose to accompany Him as He traveled from town to town throughout His three years of public ministry, perhaps even playing more sizable roles than mere accompaniment. It is the Gospel of Luke that places special emphasis on Jesus' compassion toward women (and there are many other examples to be found in the other three Gospel narratives as well), but the Old Testament accounts of the treatment of women before the time of Jesus paint a far different picture.

To truly understand and appreciate the significance of the women prophets (prophetesses) of the Old Testament, it is necessary to reflect on the multitudinous restrictions placed on the women of Israel and Judah throughout Biblical times. As was the case in most of the other cultures throughout the Mideastern world (and beyond), *patriarchy*—governance and domination by males—was the norm. It was the men who held and retained power politically, morally, economically and socially. We like to think of ourselves in today's society as more enlightened and all-inclusive in our thinking, and that is largely true. But before we become too self-congratulatory, we should remember two things: first, when our own nation was founded approximately two-and-a-half centuries ago, our own beloved

Declaration of Independence declared that "all men are created equal..." (nary a word about women, who, by the way, were not permitted to own property, vote or run for political office!), and second, even today—despite some significant inroads—women still lag appreciably behind men in terms of political representation, salary equity and upper management decision-making authority. A cigarette manufacturer targeting a female clientele once crowed, "You've come a long way, baby!" True, but there's a long way yet to go!

In their book *Every Woman in the Bible* (1999), authors Sue and Larry Richards pointed out that, "Women in the ancient Middle East were born into a man's world. During childhood and early adolescence, a woman 'belonged' to her father and was under his authority. When a woman married, she then 'belonged' to her husband. In either case, the woman's situation had to be described as 'dependent.' The father or husband was legally and economically responsible for the women in his family."

To be fair, the Old Testament seems to play "both sides against the middle" in its treatment of women, vacillating between a philosophy of equality on the one hand and a praxis of paternalism on the other. Native American tribes of the eighteenth and nineteenth centuries might accuse the authors of the Old Testament of speaking with a "forked tongue" insofar as their *view* and their *treatment* of women were often contradictory. A number of contemporary Biblical scholars such as Phyllis Trible of Union Theological Seminary and Wake Forest University and Tikva Frymer-Kensky of the University of Chicago Divinity School are of one mind that the dominant theme of the Old Testament is one of patriarchal supremacy, despite sporadic references (lip service?) to gender equality. There are many examples of seemingly contradictory rhetoric, as exemplified below.

CLASH OF CREATION STORIES

It's common knowledge that the Book of Genesis contains two separate creation myths. In the first account, God simultaneously created man and woman and made them equal in status and responsibility:

> So God created human beings, making them to be like Himself. He created them male and female, blessed them, and said, "Have many children, so that your descendants will live all over the earth and bring it under their control. I am putting you in charge of the fish, the birds, and all the wild animals." (Genesis 1:27-28)

It is clear in this creation account that neither man nor woman dominates or submits to the other. Their responsibilities of stewardship are shared and co-equal. However, the second creation account in the next chapter of Genesis paints a very different picture:

> Then the Lord God took some soil from the ground and formed a man out of it; He breathed life-giving breath into his nostrils and the man began to live....Then the Lord God placed the man in the Garden of Eden to cultivate it and to guard it. He told him, "You may eat the fruit of any tree in the garden, except the tree that gives knowledge of what is good and what is bad"...Then the Lord God said, "It is not good for the man to live alone. I will make a suitable companion to help him." So He took

some soil from the ground and formed all the animals and all the birds. Then He brought them to the man to see what he would name them; and that is how they all got their names...but not one of them was a suitable companion to help him. Then the Lord God made man fall into a deep sleep, and while he was sleeping, He took out one of the man's ribs and closed up the flesh. He formed a woman out of the rib and brought her to him. Then the man said, "At last, here is one of my own kind—bone taken from my bone, and flesh from my flesh. 'Woman' is her name because she was taken out of man."...Adam named his wife Eve, because she was the mother of all human beings. (Genesis 2:7, 15-23; 3:20)

In the second creation account, man is created first and given specific privileges and responsibilities by God. Woman is only created as an afterthought to serve as man's "helper"—and is only fashioned by God after none of the other animals has proven to be a suitable companion and aide. It is also significant that God entrusted man with the responsibility of naming all of the other creatures—including woman. The act of naming has always been a method of exerting control over what one has named. The name itself imposes limits on the identity of the one named, thereby giving the namer a semblance of control and authority. It is no accident that God's response to Moses at the theophany of the burning bush was *not* to allow Moses to use a name to describe Him:

> *Moses replied, "When I go to the Israelites and say to them, 'The God of your ancestors sent me to you,' they will ask, 'What is His name?' So what can I tell them?" God said, 'I am Who I am. You must tell them: 'The One Who is called I AM has sent me to you'." (Exodus 3:14-15)*

When we refer to God as *Yahweh*, the original Hebrew for *"I AM"*, we aren't really calling God by name as much as we are acknowledging the fact that God exists beyond all limitations and descriptions and really has no name at all.

"DUELING COMMANDMENTS"

The Ten Commandments are another example of a Biblical "mixed message." What we today call the Fourth Commandment demonstrates parental parity in terms of honor and obedience:

> Respect your father and your mother, so that you may live a long life in the land I am giving you. (Exodus 20:12)

Clearly, it is irrelevant whether one's parent is male or female. Both are equally worthy of respect from their children. And the next four Commandments that follow—injunctions against murder, adultery, theft and false accusation—are written generically enough to apply to men and women alike, free of exceptions or codicils. However, the next Commandment is much more troubling in its phraseology:

> Do not desire another man's house; do not desire his wife, his slaves, his cattle, his donkeys, or anything else that he owns. (Exodus 20:17)

How is this last Commandment to be properly interpreted? On the one hand, it lists wives alongside other possessions, thereby implying that one's wife is a personal belonging. On the other hand, wives are listed among those things cherished by husbands. So is the inclusion of the wife on this list an insult or a compliment? Does it suggest that a wife is under her husband's heel or standing atop his pedestal?

One may also wonder why this Commandment condemns the covetousness of a husband's wife but not of a wife's husband. Is not this Commandment to be followed by *all* spouses—wives and husbands—or was it written exclusively for the men? Is it possible that the wording of this Commandment—while phrased as a masculine injunction—is actually to be applied generically to all despite its sexist semantics?

OWNERSHIP OF PROPERTY

Restrictions on women went much, much further. Property was owned exclusively by men. When a father died, his property was inherited by his sons, but not by his daughters. If a father who had no sons died, then—and only then—did his unmarried daughter(s) inherit his property—but they were required to marry within the family's tribe to prevent another tribe from gaining additional land. This custom is clearly enunciated in the Book of Numbers:

> *Mahlah, Noah, Hoglah, Milcah and Tirzah were the daughters of Zelophehad, son of Hepher, son of Gilead...They went and stood before Moses, Eleazar the priest...and the whole community...and said, "Our father died...without leaving any sons...Just because he had no sons, why should our father's name disappear from Israel? Give us property among our father's relatives." Moses presented their case to the Lord, and the Lord said to him, "What the daughters of Zelophehad request is*

right; give them property among their father's relatives. Let his inheritance pass on to them. Tell the people of Israel that whenever a man dies without leaving a son, his daughter is to inherit his property.

If he has no daughter, his brothers are to inherit it. If he has no brothers, his father's brothers are to inherit it. If he has no brothers or uncles, then his nearest relative is to inherit it and hold it as his own property...just as I, the Lord, have commanded you." (Numbers 27:1-11)

This custom, or rather *commandment* from the Lord, was later modified:

The heads of the families in the clan of Gilead...said, "The Lord...commanded you to give the property of our relative Zelophehad to his daughters. But...if they marry men of another tribe, their property will then belong to that tribe, and the total allotted to us will be reduced." So Moses gave the people of Israel the following command from the Lord. He said, "...The daughters of Zelophehad are free to marry anyone they wish but only within their own tribe. The property of every Israelite will remain attached to his tribe. Every woman who inherits property in an Israelite tribe must marry a man belonging to that tribe...So Mahlah, Tirzah, Hoglah, Milcah and Noah, the daughters of Zelophehad, did as the Lord had commanded Moses, and they married their cousins...within the clans of the tribe." (Numbers 36:1-12)

Clearly it was the intention—despite this one exception—that Israelite property would be owned and administered by the men of Israel, and this custom can be traced back to Moses himself. In a similar custom, widows were not permitted to inherit their husbands' property either. The property was passed down to their sons, thus making the widows dependent on their male children.

MARRIAGE AND DIVORCE

The Old Testament wholeheartedly supports the Genesis understanding that God brings man and woman together to "become one"—and that marriage is indissoluble. Despite this idealistic outlook, Old Testament rules and conventions concerning marriage, divorce and sexuality were also unequal and restrictive toward women. Jewish law did not permit a woman to marry without her father's permission. So her marital status was not something she had control over herself—whether or not to marry, as well as the identity of her husband. This life-altering decision was left in the hands of another.

When a woman did marry, her husband had the power to divorce her at will. All he was required to do was put his intent in writing:

> *Suppose a man marries a woman and later decides that he doesn't want her, because he finds something about her that he doesn't like. So he writes out divorce papers, gives them to her, and sends her away from his home. (Deuteronomy 24:1)*

Blu Greenberg, the founder of the Jewish Orthodox Feminist Alliance, pointed out in her article "Jewish Divorce Law" in *Lilith* magazine (1977) that, "According to biblical law, a man is permitted to divorce his wife at will and send her away from his home. The second aspect highlights the biblical woman's vulnerability: economic, physical and psychological uprooting faced the woman who displeased her husband sufficiently to cause him to divorce her. She had no leverage to prevent or refuse the divorce. Neither could she divorce him."

Please note that in both the above citation from Deuteronomy and the Greenberg quotation, the phrase *"his* home" is used rather than *"their* home". This further demonstrates the property rights held by the man to the exclusion of his wife.

There is one additional codicil to Jewish marriage law that seems to favor the wife, so it would be unfair not to recognize it:

> When a man is newly married, he is not to be drafted into military service or any other public duty; he is to be excused from duty for one year, so that he can stay at home and make his wife happy. (Deuteronomy 24:5)

What is meant by "make his wife happy" is unspecified, but it is clear that some consideration is shown to the newlywed wife on this occasion.

FULFILLMENT OF PERSONAL VOWS

How many personal decisions does an individual make in one day? Hundreds? Thousands? And of the countless decisions we each make over the course of our lifetimes, none are as serious and solemn as when we vow to do something. A *vow*—stronger than a mere decision or pledge —is viewed in the

Bible as a promise made deliberately and freely to God. However, throughout the Old Testament, vows made either by an unmarried woman or by a married woman were not required to be kept unless approved by the woman's father or husband:

> When a young woman still living in her father's house makes a vow to give something to the Lord or promises to abstain from something, she must do everything that she vowed or promised unless her father raises an objection when he hears about it. But if her father forbids her to fulfill the vow when he hears about it, she is not required to keep it. The Lord will forgive her, because her father refuses to let her keep it. (Numbers 30:3-5)

> If a married woman makes a vow or promises to abstain from something, she must do everything that she vowed or promised unless her husband raises an objection when he hears about it. But if her husband forbids her to fulfill the vow when he hears about it, she is not required to keep it. The Lord will forgive her, because her husband prevented her from keeping her vow. Her husband has the right to affirm or to annul any vow or promise that she has made. (Numbers 30:10-13)

In the latter case, the husband—if he chooses to annul his wife's vow—must do so on the same day he heard of her vow, or the vow must be fulfilled. Widows and divorced women were required to keep any vows they chose to make insofar as there was no man to whom they were answerable who would be in a position to overrule them.

Note that in the second citation from Numbers the husband has the *right* to affirm or annul his wife's vows. So even the most solemn decisions made by women before God were not really their own—ratification by an associated male was required.

RITUAL PURITY

The Book of Leviticus is a legislative text that outlined the rules and regulations that largely governed the ritual sacrifices and prayer services conducted and/or administered by the priests. A number of practices were employed to return an individual to a state of cleanliness after having done something to make him or her "ritually unclean." For women, a state of ritual uncleanliness or impurity existed when a woman began to menstruate or as a result of childbirth. Invariably the impurity arose as a result of the discharge of bodily fluids.

> *When a woman has her monthly period, she remains unclean for seven days.*
>
> *Anyone who touches her remains unclean until evening. Anything on which she sits or lies during her monthly period is unclean. Anyone who touches her bed or anything on which she has sat must wash his clothes and take a bath, and he remains unclean until evening. If a man has sexual intercourse with her during her period, he is contaminated by her impurity and remains unclean for seven days, and any bed on which he lies is unclean.*
>
> *If a woman has a flow of blood for several days outside her monthly period or if her flow continues beyond her regular period, she remains unclean as long as the flow continues, just as she is during her monthly period...After her flow stops, she must wait seven days, and then she will be ritually clean.*

> On the eighth day she shall take two doves or two pigeons to the priest at the entrance to the Tent of the Lord's presence. The priest shall offer one of them as a sin offering and the other as a burnt offering, and in this way he will perform the ritual of purification for her. (Leviticus 15:19-30)

To be fair, while ritual impurity was an unclean state for women as a result of a perfectly natural biological process, a state of ritual impurity existed when men discharged semen—and this discharge resulted in identical penalties and offerings. In this case, what was "good for the goose *was* good for the gander"—or should that read "bad" rather than "good?"

Perhaps the Levitical rules governing purification after childbirth demonstrate a clear inequality of the sexes in the days of the Israelites.

> For seven days after a woman gives birth to a son, she is ritually unclean, as she is during her monthly period. On the eighth day the child shall be circumcised. Then it will be thirty-three more days until she is ritually clean from her loss of blood; she must not touch anything that is holy or enter the sacred Tent until the time of her purification is completed.
>
> For fourteen days after a woman gives birth to a daughter, she is ritually unclean, as she is during her monthly period. Then it will be sixty-six more days until she is ritually clean from her loss of blood.
>
> When the time of her purification is completed, whether for a son or daughter, she shall bring to the priest at the entrance of the Tent of the Lord's presence a one-year-old lamb for a burnt offering and a pigeon or

> *a dove for a sin offering. The priest shall present her offering to the Lord and perform the ritual to take away her impurity, and she will be ritually clean. This, then, is what a woman must do after giving birth.* (Leviticus 12:2-7)

When a woman gives birth to a daughter, she is considered ritually unclean for *twice as long* a period of time then if she had borne a son. What is the rationale behind that? And why is a woman providing animals for sacrifice as if she had sinned by giving birth? And finally—what about the husband? Should he not be party to these rituals as well? Doesn't it "take two to tango," as the saying goes? Isn't the child ultimately going to be *his* financial and vocational responsibility under the custom of the times?

As biblical scholar Phyllis Ann Bird concluded in her 1997 book *Missing Persons and Mistaken Identities: Women and Gender in Ancient Israel*, "The picture of woman obtained from the Old Testament laws can be summarized...as that of a legal nonperson; where she does become visible it is as a dependent, and usually an inferior in a male-centered and male-dominated society. The laws, by and large, do not address her, most do not even acknowledge her existence...Where ranking occurs she is always inferior to the male. Only in her role as a mother is she accorded status equal to a man's."

The Old Testament exhibited a troubling paternalism that failed in practice to treat women as equals even if it never expounded the philosophy that women were in any way less than equal. The above examples flowing all the way from the myths of creation to the day-to-day lives of the Chosen People demonstrate a mindset that relegated women to a subordinate societal position. Perhaps this will prove to make the accomplishments of the women prophets of the Old Testament all the more impressive as they were forced to raise themselves from a state of subservience to one of stature.

QUESTIONS FOR REVIEW

1. What is meant by the term *patriarchy*? How did it impact the women of ancient Israel?

2. How do the two creation accounts in Genesis differ so greatly in their treatment of "the woman?"

3. Do the Ninth and Tenth Commandments employ a double standard against women? Explain whether you agree or disagree.

4. Under what circumstances were Israelite women permitted to own property?

5. Were Israelite customs regulating marriage and divorce equally applied to men and women? Explain.

6. How binding was a vow made by a woman? Could it be overruled—and by whom?

7. What is meant by the statement "ritual impurity was an unclean state for women as a result of a perfectly natural biological process?"

8. For an Israelite mother, what was the difference—ritually—between giving birth to a son or a daughter?

Chapter Two

WHAT MAKES A PROPHETESS "PROPHETIC?"

Languages can be fascinating to study, and this is especially so when they are compared with one another.

Sometimes a word in one language has an opposite or contradictory meaning in another. Some words in the same language have a multitude of meanings—words like "just" and "spirit" immediately come to mind—and homonyms, or "sound-alike words," can be fun, too.

This, of course, brings us to the key word in this volume —*prophet*. It can be defined rather broadly or can be used in a very restrictive sense as well. Many people equate the word "prophet" with "predictor" because the related word "prophecy" implies prognostication of future events. If someone were to predict that a certain baseball team would win tomorrow's game or a certain political candidate would win an upcoming election, do these accurate predictions entitle the person to be labeled a "prophet?" Must one demonstrate an accuracy of prediction over a protracted period of time to earn that designation? Does prophethood imply a certain level of accurate guesswork—or does it require qualities or a calling of a much deeper or higher nature?

Our English word *prophet* is derived from the Greek word *prophete*, which is a translation of the Hebrew word *navi*, which means "one who speaks for another"—in this case, one who speaks for God. In Hebrew, the feminine form of this word is *neviah*. To be an Old Testament *navi/neviah* or *prophete* or *prophet/ess* did not necessarily suggest that one would be predicting future events—although many of the Biblical prophets *did* do that—but rather defined that person as one who had been entrusted by God to deliver His messages to the Chosen People. On occasion, those messages were indeed predictive, but many times they were not. But they *always* had a divine component lying at the heart of their messages.

While this understanding of the word *prophet* eliminates some of its broader usages, it doesn't quite "pin it down" specifically enough. If a person—man or woman—is to be considered an authentic prophet, how is that designation determined?

Dr. Wilda C. Gafney, a professor of Hebrew and Old Testament Studies at the Lutheran Theological Seminary in Philadelphia, offered a very viable definition in her excellent and comprehensive text *Daughters of Miriam: Women Prophets in Ancient Israel* (2008): "The simple definition of prophecy with which I am working is that prophecy is the proclamation and/or performance of a divine word by a religious intermediary to an individual or community." Dr. Gafney went on to list some of these proclamations and performances, which included "engaging in intercessory prayer, dancing, drumming, singing, giving and interpreting laws, delivering oracles on behalf of YHWH (sometimes in ecstasy, sometimes demonstratively), resolving disputes, working wonders, mustering troops and fighting battles, archiving their oracles in writing, and experiencing visions." Clearly, the parameters of prophetic behavior and ministry are quite broad. I think that is an important consideration to bear in mind when determining who is—or is not—an authentic prophet.

In some cases, Scripture quotes God (or perhaps another Biblical figure) as identifying an individual as an authentic prophet, as was the case with Jeremiah:

> *The Lord said to me, "I chose you before I gave you life, and before you were born I selected you to be a* prophet *to the nations." (Jeremiah 1:4)*

At other times, while Scripture does not specifically employ the word *prophet*, it records an instance of God calling an individual to deliver a message—the primary definitional role of a prophet. So even if the word *prophet* is not employed, we recognize from the person's assignment and responsibilities that he/she is serving God in that capacity. An example of this is Isaiah of Jerusalem:

> *Then I heard the Lord say, "Whom shall I send? Who will be Our messenger?" I answered, "I will go! Send me!" So He told me to go and give the people this message... (Isaiah 6:8-9)*

Lastly, it is important to recognize and acknowledge the contributions made by other extra-Biblical sources to our understanding and appreciation of the Old Testament and its messages. The written text of the *Hebrew Scriptures*, or Old Testament, has been supplemented in Judaism with a legislative corpus known as the *Talmud*. The *Talmud* is a compilation of the laws of Judaism that had previously been passed down orally (along with commentary and explanation from leading rabbis) from generation to generation. It was first compiled around 220 CE by the esteemed Rabbi Judah ha-Nasi ("Judah the Prince") and contained two parts: the *Mishnah* (a listing of the variegated Jewish laws) and the *Gemara*, (the rabbinic discussion and explanation of these laws). This legislative opus is referred to as the *Palestinian Talmud* (the word "Talmud" means "learning"), but several centuries later, circa 500 CE, another, more extensive Talmud was composed and published in Babylonia, which had become a major Jewish center for Scriptural studies. Fittingly, this second Talmud became known as the *Babylonian Talmud*, and has become the "go to" book concerning Jewish laws and customs globally since its compilation.

In his book *The Concise Guide to Judaism: History, Practice, Faith* (1990), Rabbi Roy A. Rosenberg of the Temple of Universal Judaism in New York pointed out that "The *Babylonian Talmud* is the major text studied in rabbinic academies to this day anywhere in the world. Thus, when a Jew refers to 'Talmud,' he means the one produced in Babylonia...It is referred to as 'the sea of the Talmud,' and every Jew who is capable of doing so is urged to 'search in it, and search in it again, for everything is contained in it' (Abot 5:22)."

Why is it necessary to mention the *Talmud* at this point? In addition to the women in the Old Testament who are labeled prophets (or prophetesses) and those who clearly have performed some of the duties of prophets while not being identified as such specifically, the Talmud also designates several additional women as prophets. For the purposes of this book, and to clarify this book's definition of the word *prophet*, it is women from among these three groups whose lives and ministries we will discuss. Perhaps Professor Claude Mariottini of the Northern Baptist Seminary explained it best in his 2013 blog post entitled "Women Prophets in the Hebrew Bible" when he wrote, "While there are almost thirty men who are called prophets in the Old Testament, there are only five women who are called prophetesses...Miriam (Exodus 15:20), Deborah (Judges 4:4), Huldah (2 Kings 22:14), Noadiah (Nehemiah 6:14), and Isaiah's wife (Isaiah 8:3), a woman whose name is not given by Isaiah." Mariottini goes on to explain, "According to the Rabbis, these five women were not the only women prophets in Israel. The *Talmud* (Megillah 14a) mentions four other women who were considered prophetesses. These four women were Sarah, Hannah, Abigail and Esther." While the Talmud specified these four women as prophets, it failed to include in its list either Isaiah's wife ("the prophetess") or Noadiah. This book will include all nine of these women as well as several other women whose designation as prophetesses is, in sports jargon, "on the bubble," or open to further discussion.

We will examine all of them—and some other possibilities as well.

QUESTIONS FOR REVIEW

1. What is meant by the term "prophet"? Where does this word come from?

2. Is the prediction of future events an essential component of being a prophet?

3. How does Dr. Wilda C. Gafney describe the parameters of prophethood?

4. What is the *Talmud*—and what does it have to say about the women prophets of the Hebrew Scriptures?

5. Are the same women recognized as prophetesses in Christianity and Judaism?

ACKNOWLEDGED PROPHETS

Chapter Three
SARAH

Even a casual reader of Scripture knows something of Sarah, the wife of Abraham and one of the most well-known women in the Old Testament. If Abraham can aptly be described as the "Father of the Chosen People," then it is only right to christen Sarah as the "Mother of the Chosen People." But does this designation necessarily mean that Sarah should be considered a prophetess? The text of the *Hebrew Scriptures* never defines Sarah as such, but the *Talmud*—the compendium of commentary by reputable and scholarly rabbis on the *Hebrew Scriptures*—does. Is this justifiable?

Sarah appeared exclusively in the Book of Genesis (although she is also mentioned much later in several of the books of the New Testament), so chronologically she would be the first woman to grace the pages of this text. The first citation we read of her is this:

> Abram [Abraham] *married Sarai {Sarah], and Nahor married Milcah, the daughter of Haran, who was also the father of Iscah. Sarai was not able to have children."* (Genesis 11:29-30)

SARAH: WIFE, HALF-SISTER, BEAUTY

It wasn't until later in Genesis that we receive more detailed information about the exact relationship between Abraham and Sarah. Abraham, in discussing Sarah with King Abimelech of Gerar, revealed:

> *She really is my sister. She is the daughter of my father, but not of my mother, and I married her."* (Genesis 20:12)

So it turns out that Abraham and Sarah were half-brother and half-sister—not a tidbit of information that is concealed in Scripture, but one that is not given much prominence, either.

You may recall that Abraham capitalized on this fact on several parallel occasions. The first instance was when God called on Abraham, who was originally named Abram before God changed his name, to leave his home and his life in urban Ur, a city of the Chaldees (now part of southern Iraq). Eventually Sarai's name would be changed to Sarah, as well. When Abraham entered Canaan with his entire household, they experienced a prolonged and intensive famine that forced them to continue south of Canaan to the land of Egypt.

Sarah was apparently quite beautiful, so Abraham made a strange request of her:

> When the Egyptians see you, they will assume that you are my wife, and so they will kill me and let you live. Tell them that you are my sister; then because of you they will let me live and treat me well. (Genesis 12:12-13)

This deception accomplished its objective. When news of Sarah's beauty was brought to the King of Egypt, he took Sarah as his wife, not only sparing Abraham's life, but gifting him with flocks of sheep, goats, cattle, donkeys, camels—and slaves. However:

> Because the king had taken Sarah, the Lord sent terrible diseases on him and on the people of his palace. Then the king sent for Abram and asked him, "What have you done to me? Why didn't you tell me that she was your wife? Why did you say that she was your sister, and let me take her as my wife? Here is your wife; take her and get out!" (Genesis 12:17-19)

Upon their expulsion from Egypt, the now wealthy Abraham and Sarah traveled north to the land of Canaan, where Abraham and Sarah settled in Hebron, a city that is nestled in the Judean Mountains about 19 miles south of Jerusalem. It was here that God made a solemn pledge to Abraham:

> ...Your only son will be your heir...Look at the sky and try to count the stars; you will have as many descendants as that. (Genesis 15:4-5)

A SLAVE SUBSTITUTE

It seems that this promise was not fulfilled in the short term, and when Abraham and Sarah were still childless a decade later, Sarah took the initiative to address the situation:

> *Abram's wife Sarai had not borne him any children. But she had an Egyptian slave girl named Hagar, and so she said to Abram, "The Lord has kept me from having children. Why don't you sleep with my slave girl? Perhaps she can have a child for me." Abram agreed with what Sarai said. So she gave Hagar to him to be his concubine...Abram had intercourse with Hagar, and she became pregnant. (Genesis 16:1-4)*

It should be noted that the intimate relationship between Abraham and Hagar was not considered adulterous or in any way inappropriate according to the social mores of the era. In fact, since Hagar was considered the property of Sarah, Sarah, rather than Hagar, was considered to be the legal mother of Hagar's infant. However, Hagar's pregnancy did not cause Sarah and Hagar to bond over a shared joy. Rather, Genesis records just the opposite:

> *When she [Hagar] found out that she was pregnant, she became proud and despised Sarai. Then Sarai said to Abram, It's your fault that Hagar despises me. I myself gave her to you, and ever since she found out that she was pregnant, she has despised me. May the Lord judge which one of us is right, you or me." (Genesis 16:4-5)*

Since Hagar was the property of Sarah, Sarah was empowered to discipline and command Hagar as she saw fit. So Sarah treated her so cruelly that the pregnant Hagar ran away from Abram's compound, until an angel persuaded her to return.

> He said, "Go back to her and be her slave." Then he said, "I will give you so many descendants that no one will be able to count them. You are going to have a son, and you will name him Ishmael [which means 'God hears'], because the Lord has heard your cry of distress." (Genesis 16:9-11)

Upon her return, Hagar gave birth to a son and named him Ishmael, as the angel commanded. Abraham was 86 years old at the time. It wasn't until another thirteen years had passed that God made a covenant with him that had a profound impact on both Abraham and Sarah:

> When Abram was ninety-nine years old, the Lord appeared to him and said, "I am the Almighty God. Obey me and always do what is right. I will make My covenant with you and give you many descendants... Your name will no longer be Abram, but Abraham, because I am making you the ancestor of many nations...
>
> The whole land of Canaan will belong to your descendants forever, and I will be their God...You must no longer call your wife Sarai; from now on her name is Sarah [which means "princess"]. I will bless her and I will give you a son by her...she will become the mother of nations, and there will be kings among her descendants." (Genesis 17:1-2,4-6,8,15-16)

As delighted as he was, Abraham asked God for further clarification:

> *Abraham bowed down with his face touching the ground, but he began to laugh when he thought, "Can a man have a child when he is a hundred years old? Can Sarah have a child at ninety?" He asked God, "Why not let Ishmael be my heir?"*
>
> *But God said, "No. Your wife Sarah will bear you a son and you will name him Isaac [which means "he laughs"]. I will keep My covenant with him and his descendants forever. It is an everlasting covenant...I will keep My covenant with your son Isaac, who will be born to Sarah about this time next year." When God finished speaking to Abraham, He left him. (Genesis 17:17-22)*

A PROMISE FULFILLED

Sarah did give birth to Isaac the following year, and the child was circumcised on the eighth day, according to custom. But a final confrontation between Sarah and Hagar was still in the offing. On the day that Isaac was weaned—that's to say, he had ceased nursing and was prepared to take other means of sustenance, probably around the age of three or four—Abraham hosted a great feast. But this feast served as the setting for the last clash between the "mothers of Ishmael"—legal and biological.

Sue and Larry Richards' text *Every Woman in the Bible* (1999) described this latest incident as a virtual ultimatum issued to Abraham by Sarah. "At the party Sarah saw Ishmael teasing Isaac [the *NKJV* says 'scoffing']. Sarah exploded and demanded that Abraham 'cast out this bondwoman and her son.' Her reference to 'the son of this bondwoman' shows both that the relationship of the two women was still marked by hostility, and that Sarah had little or no affection for Ishmael." Yet, the *Good News Bible* both softens and embellishes this incident:

> ...Ishmael, whom Hagar the Egyptian had borne to Abraham, was playing with Sarah's son Isaac. Sarah saw them and said to Abraham, "Send this slave girl and her son away. The son of this woman must not get any part of your wealth, which my son Isaac should inherit." This troubled Abraham very much, because Ishmael also was his son. But God said to Abraham, "Don't be worried about the boy and your slave Hagar. Do whatever Sarah tells you, because it is through Isaac that you will have the descendants I have promised. I will also give many children to the son of the slave girl, so that they will become a nation. He too is your son." (Genesis 21:9-13)

It would appear from this demand of Sarah's that her primary interest in expelling Hagar and Ishmael was financial—to secure all of Abraham's wealth for her own son. And God, recognizing Abraham's conflicting emotions, placated him with the promise that Hagar and Ishmael would not suffer from deprivation.

The final reference to Sarah in the Book of Genesis simply chronicles her obituary:

> Sarah lived to be 127 years old. She died in Hebron in the land of Canaan, and Abraham mourned her death. (Genesis 23:1-2)

Does the story of Sarah begin and end here? If the answer is an affirmative one, then the Book of Genesis—at least in the way it is translated in the *Good News Bible*—offers little evidence to support the description of Sarah as a prophetess. The text of the Old Testament does not define her as such, and Dr. Gafney's detailed understanding of the parameters of prophethood (as described in Chapter 2) doesn't seem to apply to Sarah, either. She doesn't explicitly exhibit any of the behaviors that are usually associated with the delivery of messages or even the foretelling of future events. Yet Judaism does indeed view Sarah as a prophetess—and a very important one at that—and there are multiple reasons for defining her as such.

SARAH THE "YISKAH"

Rabbi Shalom Goodman of the Mayanot Institute of Jewish Studies in Jerusalem pointed out in www.chabad.org that "Sarah also had another name—*Yiskah* ("Jessica"), meaning "Seer"—because she was a prophetess and had the ability to see into the future." He even suggested that "God told Abraham to listen to Sarah, because she was a greater prophet than he." On the same website, Rabbi Goodman credited Sarah with joining Abraham as God's messenger, describing her as "instrumental in teaching thousands of people about monotheism—the belief in one God" and maintaining that "Abraham would guide the men, while Sarah influenced the women…"

Dr. Tamar Kadari, dean of the Schechter Institute of Jewish Studies, in discussing on the website www.jwa.org the *midrashim* (a series of ancient commentaries on the Hebrew Scriptures), suggested that they present Sarah "as a prophet and a righteous woman whose actions are worthy of emulation; she converted Gentiles and drew them into the bosom of Judaism." As discussed above in Chapter 21 of Genesis, "Abraham was ennobled through her, and subordinated himself to her; God commanded him to heed his wife, because of her prophetic power."

Certainly these esteemed scholars feel quite comfortable with the concept that Sarah's name be included in the roster of prophetesses of the *Hebrew Scriptures*. They see her not only as a prophetess, but as a leader, role model and missionary. Perhaps Dina Coopersmith of the Midreshet Rachel Seminary in Israel can add yet another layer to this understanding of Sarah—that of deep thinker and forward planner—in her analysis of Sarah on the website www.aish.com. After reviewing and analyzing external material and commentary found in the Hebrew Scriptures and Talmud, Ms. Coopersmith arrived at several insightful conclusions which, hopefully, are summarized here with accuracy.

First, Sarah's other name, Yiskah, according to the great eleventh-century French rabbi Rashi (real name Shlomo Yitzchaki), has three important meanings: (1) that Sarah was imbued with the "Divine Spirit," (2) that she was blessed with striking physical beauty, and (3) that she possessed great leadership ability.

Second, again according to Rashi, Sarah had, "the voice of Divine insight in her [so] we learn that Sarah superseded Abraham in prophecy."

Third, putting ego aside, Sarah took the initiative to offer Hagar to Abraham as the bearer of his child, only coming to realize after Hagar conceived that her pregnancy was only the result of a "miscommunication" between Abraham with God. Abraham had complained to God that:

> *I have no children...My only heir is Eliezer of Damascus. You have given me no children and one of my slaves will inherit my property.* (Genesis 15:2-3)

Sarah, after questioning Abraham about this conversation, realized that Hagar's pregnancy occurred because Abraham said "*my* only heir, *me* no children, and *my* property" in his plea to God, rather than broadening his vocabulary to "*our* children, *us* no children, and *our* property" in phraseology that would have included Sarah in the equation. Even if Abraham had hoped or assumed he'd have a child with Sarah, his vocabulary was less inclusive. But, as Ms. Coopersmith concluded, "What was done was done. Ishmael was born. He was still Abraham's son, educated and loved by Abraham."

Fourth, Ms. Coopersmith posits that, "Had Sarah known about this omission, she would have...sent him back to re-ask, and the whole gut-wrenching Hagar episode could have been avoided. Sarah prophesied this would have far-reaching horrific effects for the Jewish people; Ishmael became the forbearer of the Arab nation that in the future would violently compete for the land of Israel. No wonder Sarah was angry."

And lastly, Ms. Coopersmith also maintains that after Sarah gave birth to Isaac years later, Isaac grew up in the same environment where Ishmael had begun to involve himself in "dangerous and immoral behavior...building altars and offering sacrifices for idol worship." If this were indeed occurring, it would only be sensible for Sarah to want to shield Isaac from such unsavory pursuits, and would explain God's words to Abraham:

> Do whatever Sarah tells you, because it is through Isaac that you will have the descendants I have promised. (Genesis 21:12)

The conclusion that is drawn here is a tribute to Sarah's foresight. She was able to project far into the future and see, as Ms. Coopersmith concludes, that, "If Isaac would be influenced by this person [Ishmael], the Jewish nation's genetic make-up would be in danger! ...Sarah, with clear-sighted vision and a discerning ability to analyze and prioritize, was able to establish the foundations of her home and nation with determination and strength."

So, is it appropriate to consider Sarah a prophetess? The evidence gleaned from different sources of Jewish scholarship would certainly view the title as justified.

QUESTIONS FOR REVIEW

1. Why did Abraham—on two separate occasions—ask Sarah to claim to be his sister rather than his wife?

2. Why did Sarah offer her slave Hagar to Abraham to help him to produce an heir?

3. How old was Abraham when he sired Ishmael? How old were Abraham and Sarah when Isaac was born?

4. What is Rabbi Goodman's justification for defining Sarah as a prophetess?

5. According to one theory, how did the use of the word "my" rather than "our" lead to the pregnancy of Hagar?

6. What unacceptable behaviors is it possible that the young Ishmael was exhibiting to cause Sarah to request his expulsion?

Chapter Four
MIRIAM

There is, perhaps, no greater or more highly esteemed figure in the Old Testament than Moses, who led the Chosen People out of slavery in Egypt. Anyone who has ever studied any aspect of soteriology is familiar with Moses, who is revered as both a prophet and a Patriarch of the Israelites. It is to Moses that the composition of the *Torah* (the first five books of the Old Testament, a.k.a. *the Pentateuch*) is usually ascribed (even if he didn't personally compose it word-for-word himself), and the details of his life most students of the Judeo-Christian-Islamic tradition can recite by heart. He is truly one of the towering figures of Scripture.

While the purpose of this chapter is to discuss the prophetess Miriam, the sister of Moses, it is difficult to discuss her prophetic ministry without giving sufficient attention to the details of Moses' life as well, since the story of the two of them is so intrinsically intertwined.

Personal information about the family life and upbringing of Moses and Miriam is rather scant, with the exception of several Biblical stories of note. Religious authors Sue and Larry Richards, in their book *Every Woman in the Bible* (1999), identified the parents of Moses and Miriam: "Jochabed was of the family of Levi, the third son of Leah and Jacob. She married her brother Kohath's oldest son, Amram. They had three children, Miriam, Aaron and Moses, all of whom distinguished themselves among God's chosen."

No other children of Jochabed and Amram are mentioned in Scripture, and it is generally thought that Miriam was the eldest child, perhaps seven to ten years older than Moses, while brother Aaron was the middle child. The dates of the births of these children have never been accurately determined, but historical records would suggest that all three were born in the early 1300's BCE. At this time, the Israelites, whose ancestors had been invited to move to Egypt from Canaan by their forefather Joseph, had been relegated to a state of slavery by an Egyptian Pharaoh who had grown fearful of their increasing numbers and affluence as "aliens" living in his kingdom. The word *Hebrew*, which is often used as a synonym for *Israelite*, is derivative of the Egyptian word *apiru*, meaning laborer, servant or slave. History is also unclear as to the identity of the Egyptian Pharaoh who enslaved the Israelites (or Hebrew/apiru), but the time frame would suggest either Seti I or Ramses II as the likely despot.

At the time of Moses' birth, the Pharaoh, fearing the burgeoning number of Israelites in his midst, chose to address this "crisis" in a rather heartless manner:

> Finally the king issued a command to all his people: "Take every newborn Hebrew boy and throw him into the Nile, but let all the girls live." (Exodus 1:22)

Since Moses' older brother had already been born before this decree took effect, he was safe, but the infant Moses was not. Jochabed concealed Moses from prying Egyptian eyes for three months, but realized it would be necessary to take alternative steps to protect him:

> When she could not hide him any longer, she took a basket made of reeds and covered it with tar to make it watertight. She put the baby in it and then placed it in the tall grass at the edge of the river. The baby's sister [Miriam] stood some distance away to see what would happen to him. (Exodus 2:3-4)

MIRIAM THE "SAVIOR"

It is at this juncture that Miriam first asserts her great value as an instrument of God's Providence. No one knows the length of time that the infant Moses was hidden in the basket among the shoreline bulrushes of the Nile. It may have been days, weeks—or even months. But Miriam was entrusted with the responsibility of serving as a sentinel for her baby brother to keep him safe—a responsibility she clearly took very seriously. When Moses' basket was discovered by Pharaoh's daughter and her maidservants—an occurrence over which Miriam had no control—it was her cleverness, understanding and quick wit that prevented a possible catastrophe from unfolding.

> *The king's daughter came down to the river to bathe, while her servants walked along the bank. Suddenly she noticed the basket in the tall grass and sent a slave girl to get it. The princess opened it and saw a baby boy. He was crying, and she felt sorry for him. "This is one of the Hebrew babies," she said.* (Exodus 2:5-6)

Even though Scripture records that the daughter of Pharaoh looked upon the child with compassion, Miriam, nearby and hiding, could not possibly have known the princess' next steps. Knowing of her father's injunction, it's quite possible that the princess may have chosen simply to throw the child back into the water. But Miriam immediately revealed herself and approached Pharaoh's daughter. In *Every Woman in the Bible*, Sue and Larry Richards also pointed out that the more affluent women in most Middle Eastern cultures at the time commonly employed other lower class women to serve as domestic wet nurses, thus relieving them of a maternal function they found to be tedious. So Miriam asked the princess:

> *Shall I go and call a Hebrew woman to nurse the baby for you?* (Exodus 2:7)

We will never know if the princess was intent on sparing the infant Moses or not, and it's quite possible that Miriam's timely question may have planted a seed of thought in the mind of the princess to disregard her father's decree and spare the baby. In any event, after Miriam approached the princess with her question, the princess' response must surely have overjoyed and relieved Miriam:

"Please do," she answered. (Exodus 2:8)

Miriam brought her mother Jochabed before the princess, and the princess then commissioned her:

"Take this baby and nurse him for me, and I will pay you." So she [Jochabed] took the baby and nursed him. Later, when the child was old enough, she took him to the king's daughter, who adopted him as her own son. (Exodus 2:9-10)

Certainly Pharaoh's decree to execute all male Hebrew infants was a heinous and barbaric act, but it was through the subterfuge of Jochabed and the quick thinking of Miriam that Moses was able to survive this particular case of infanticide. What should not be lost in this episode is that Miriam showed such great insight and maturity when she was still quite young —somewhere between the ages of seven and ten. Quite an accomplishment for one at such a tender age!

The story of Moses from this point on is very well known: he grew up as a member of Pharaoh's court but never forgot his Israelite roots. Upon seeing an Egyptian overlord kill a Hebrew slave, he, in turn, reciprocated by killing the Egyptian. When the homicide he committed as retribution was discovered, he fled to the land of Midian, which, according to Professor of Archaeology William G. Dever, was located in the "northwest Arabian Peninsula, on the east shore of the Gulf of Aqaba on the Red Sea." In Midian, Moses met the family of a priest named Jethro, whose daughter Zipporah he married. Years passed, and while Moses was herding the sheep and goats of his father-in-law across the desert at Mount Sinai, Moses encountered God in the theophany of the burning bush. At Sinai, God commissioned Moses to lead the Israelites out of captivity in Egypt—and Moses, like so many subsequent prophets, resisted this divine assignment. After the Lord reassured him and gave him several miraculous abilities to demonstrate his worthiness (as well as permitting him to use his brother Aaron for moral and verbal support), Moses approached Pharaoh, who promptly rejected his request and began to treat the Israelite slaves even more harshly.

God afflicted the Egyptians with a series of plagues to demonstrate His ultimate power: turning the Nile River into blood, infesting the land with frogs, gnats, flies and locusts, killing the domesticated pack animals and herds, infecting the Egyptians with boils, sending three days of profound darkness, and finally —the killing of each first-born Egyptian son in what is known today as the first *Pesach* (Passover) event. This final plague forced Pharaoh's hand, and he capitulated. But as the Israelites departed Egypt by crossing the Red Sea (or, more probably, a marshland known as the "sea of reeds"), he sent his troops to re-capture them to continue their lives of slavery.

Chapter 14 of Exodus recorded the ensuing miracle. Moses lifted his staff above his head and the waters of the sea parted to allow the Israelites to cross safely to the other side. When the Egyptian army tried to pursue them, Moses again extended his hand over the sea, and the waters returned to their original state, drowning all of the Egyptian troops—and freeing the Israelites from their bondage. The Israelites, many of whom had been skeptical—even downright mistrustful of Moses' leadership and divine commission—were now awestruck at the power of God as well as His deliverance of them from slavery.

MIRIAM THE MUSICIAN

Chapter 15 of Exodus describes how Moses and his Israelite followers sang a song ("the Song of Moses") that praised God for His great power in saving them and extolled Him as their King forever. But this song was immediately followed by another song—which put Moses' sister center stage:

> *The prophet Miriam, Aaron's sister, took her tambourine, and all the women followed her, playing tambourines and dancing. Miriam sang for them:*
>
> *"Sing to the Lord, because He has won a glorious victory; He has thrown the horses and their riders into the sea." (Exodus 15:20-21)*

This second Scriptural reference to Miriam (following her protection of the infant Moses in the Nile River many years earlier) is incredibly short in duration, but nevertheless has a great deal to say. First, it specifically identifies Miriam as a prophet. Second, it shows her support of her brother and both her acknowledgment of the power of God as well as the importance she places on conveying her faith publicly. Lastly, through her music and lyrics she clearly demonstrates her leadership within the Israelite community—especially among the women. As Dr. Gafney previously reminded us—singing, dancing and playing musical instruments can all be elements used by a prophet in his/her ministry.

MIRIAM REPRIMANDED AND PUNISHED

The final mention of Miriam's ministry in Sacred Scripture further reflected her calling as a prophet, but was accompanied by a severe reprimand and, hopefully, an important lesson learned. This last incident is rather perplexing—and is open to several different interpretations. It addresses Moses' marriage, Miriam's jealousy and the respective roles of Moses, Miriam and Aaron—roles that were prophetic, yet unequal.

> *Moses had married a Cushite woman and Miriam and Aaron criticized him for it.*
>
> *They said, "Has the Lord spoken only through Moses? Hasn't He also spoken through us?" The Lord heard what they said. (Moses was a humble man, more humble than anyone else on earth.)*
>
> *Suddenly the Lord said to Moses, Aaron and Miriam, "I want the three of you to come out to the Tent of My Presence." They went, and the Lord came down in a pillar of cloud, stood at the entrance of the Tent, and called out, "Aaron! Miriam!" The two of them stepped forward, and the Lord said, "Now hear what I have to say! When there are prophets among you, I reveal myself to them in visions and speak to them in dreams. It is different when I speak with My servant Moses; I have put him in charge of all My people Israel. So I speak to him face-to-face, clearly and not in riddles; he has even seen My form! How dare you speak against My servant Moses?"*
>
> *The Lord was angry with them; and so as He departed...Miriam's skin was suddenly covered with a dreaded disease and turned as white as snow...So Moses cried out to the Lord, "Oh God, heal her!" The Lord*

answered, "If her father had spit in her face, she would have to bear her disgrace for seven days. So let her be shut out of the camp for a week, and after that she can be brought back in." Miriam was shut out of the camp for seven days, and the people did not move on until she was brought back in. (Numbers 12:1-16)

It is unclear in the first line of the above citation exactly why Miriam and Aaron were unhappy with Moses' marriage. It is also unclear if the siblings were critical of Moses' marriage to Zipporah, the daughter of the Midianite priest Jethro, or if either Zipporah had died or Moses had divorced her—and remarried. We know that Zipporah and their two sons Gershom and Eliezer were not in Egypt during the time of the plagues and the Exodus event, because Jethro brought Zipporah, Gershom and Eliezer to Moses when the Israelites camped in the desert after their escape from Pharaoh's forces (Exodus 18:1-5). The citation mentions that Moses married a Cushite woman (Zipporah is identified as Midianite), but the Biblical land of Cush has never been clearly defined or located with geographic precision. It is usually described as a land that may have existed on either side—or both sides—of the Red Sea, so it could be synonymous with Midian. So it begs the question: were Miriam and Aaron critical of Moses' marriage to Zipporah —or did he have another spouse?

The question really matters very little in that it only serves as an excuse for the larger controversy that was to follow. Miriam and Aaron, who were both called by God to serve as His prophets, had become jealous of Moses' special status in God's eyes. In speaking out critically of Moses' behavior, they demonstrated that they believed themselves to be equal to Moses in stature, and hoped to achieve some sort of parity with him. Miriam, the older sister, clearly took the lead here (which is why her name is mentioned first), and she and Aaron were immediately reprimanded by God, Who made it clear that Moses had been given unique, personal responsibilities that differentiated him from them—and placed him in a position where his siblings had no right to question him.

However, the reprimand did not end with either a stiff warning or a "slap on the wrist." Miriam paid a price for her jealousy and impudence when God plagued her with a case of leprosy. At Moses' request, Miriam's leprosy lasted for only one week—a week that necessitated her leaving the Israelite camp so as not to infect its members. Aaron escaped punishment, it is thought, not because he was male, but because, in his role as high priest, he had to be available to the people to supervise the rites and rituals of worship that were offered daily. While it was important that the Israelites continued to move forward to the Promised Land that awaited them, it was a real tribute to Miriam that the Chosen People opted not to move forward at all until Miriam was permitted to re-join them.

When the word "prophet" is employed, the word is usually followed by images of highly charismatic and dynamic individuals either preaching passionately or performing miracles with great dramatic flourish. The behaviors exhibited by Miriam don't, on face value, seem to "fit the mold." She really doesn't ever do these things—at least, not to our knowledge. But her prophetic ministry really does open up the parameters of what it means to serve as a messenger of God. Miriam displayed great love and stewardship for her baby brother Moses, and most probably saved his life through her watchfulness and quick thinking. She later led the Israelites in worship through song and dance when it was so necessary for them to offer thanks, praise and adoration to God. Later, even in adversity, she taught future generations a valuable lesson about envy and its consequences when allowed to take root. Not really a bad ministry!

QUESTIONS FOR REVIEW

1. What do we know about the composition of Moses' family?

2. In what way did Miriam's quick thinking possibly save the life of the infant Moses?

3. What is the significance of Miriam's musical tribute to God after the Israelites crossed the Red Sea into freedom?

4. Why were Miriam and Aaron reprimanded by God—and why was Miriam (but not Aaron) punished?

5. Why did the Israelites refuse to continue on their journey to Canaan until Miriam was able to re-join them?

Chapter Five

DEBORAH

*I*n his first letter to the Corinthians, St. Paul discussed the gifts bestowed on different individuals by the Holy Spirit and how these gifts each make unique contributions that other gifts are simply unable to provide:

> There are different kinds of spiritual gifts, but the same Spirit gives them.
>
> There are different ways of serving, but the same Lord is served. There are different abilities to perform service, but the same God gives ability to all for their particular service. (1 Corinthians 12:4-6)

While he probably wasn't doing so, Paul could have written these words after contemplating on the unique roles played by Miriam and Deborah for the greater good of the Israelites. For while Miriam and Deborah both serve as prophetesses during

Old Testament times, their respective gifts and ministries were quite different.

When Moses died immediately prior to leading the Israelites across the River Jordan into the land of Canaan, the mantle of leadership was passed to his assistant/lieutenant Joshua. When Joshua and the Israelites arrived in Canaan, they discovered that other tribes had settled there since their forefather and Patriarch Jacob had vacated the land with the rest of his family to join his son Joseph in Egypt. So this entry into Canaan earmarked a new era in Israelite history known as the "Age of Judges." This time period extended approximately from 1250 BCE to the anointing of King Saul in 1030 BCE—220 years.

The Age of Judges was a unique time in Israelite history for several reasons. First, the Chosen People were not really a united nation; rather, they were, at best, a loose confederation of related tribes. Second, unlike the other Canaanite tribes around them (Phoenicians, Philistines, Ammonites, Moabites, Perizzites, Hittites, Hivites, Jebusites, Edomites, etc.), the Israelites had no central government, which would have existed had they been under some kind of monarchical rule. They were loosely administered by individuals known as "judges," whose primary function was not necessarily judicial in nature. Today, when we think of judges, we visualize them presiding in courtrooms for purposes of adjudication and legal interpretation. The judges of Israel during this period, according to Rabbi Roy A. Rosenberg in *The Concise Guide to Judaism: History, Practice, Faith* (1990), "were not judicial figures, but instead charismatic leaders in war against various non-Israelite tribes." Daniel Smith-Christopher, in his 2005 text *The Old Testament: Our Call to*

Faith and Justice, further defined the Israelite judge of this time period as "one who acted as a temporary military leader, as well as arbiter of disputes within and between tribes. Judges were also expected to remind the people of their responsibilities to God."

The truth is that the jurisdiction or influence of some of the judges did not really extend to all of the Israelite tribes. To varying degrees, their loose leadership could have been either narrow or extensive. Hebrew Scripture lists the following as judges: Joshua, Othniel, Ehud, Shamgar, Deborah, Gideon, Tola, Jair, Jephthah, Ibzan, Elon, Abdon, Samson and Samuel, and it was their leadership (in the order listed above) that predated the establishment of an Israelite monarchy under King Saul in 1030 BCE.

JUDGE, PROPHET, WIFE

Deborah was the fifth in a roster of 14 judges, and she stands out both as the only woman and as one of only two judges who "doubled" as prophets (the other being Samuel). The Book of Judges chronicles the exploits of most of these leaders, and Gideon and Samson probably stand out as the most recognizable names. Deborah is only mentioned in chapters 4 and 5 of the Book of Judges, which are silent about many of the important details of her life.

> *Now Deborah, the wife of Lappidoth, was a prophet, and she was serving as a judge for the Israelites at that time. She would sit under a certain palm tree between Ramah and Bethel in the hill country of*

> Ephraim, and the people of Israel would go there for her decisions.
> (Judges 4:4-5)

This two-verse passage about Deborah says both a little and a lot. It identifies Deborah as both a prophet and a judge, and it demonstrates that Deborah was so well-respected as an arbiter that people would travel great distances to consult her for her judgments. It also identifies her as a married woman. But the passage offers no insight into her "call narrative" (the circumstances under which she was commissioned by God to serve as His prophetess), nor does it explain the circumstances under which she ascended to the "rank" of judge. Given the fact that Israelite women during this time were usually entrusted with domestic, household responsibilities while the men handled spiritual, political and economic concerns, it would be very enlightening to understand the events that led to her ascendancy. Clearly, there must have been either some type of public divine revelation or a cataclysmic precipitating event that elevated Deborah in the eyes of her people to be so well-respected.

However, an alternative theory may shed some light on this subject. In her 2008 text *Kabbalistic Teachings of the Female Prophets*, author and social justice activist J. Zohara Meyerhoff-Hieronimus posited that, "Deborah...was independently wealthy; she owned palm trees in Jericho, orchards in Ramah, oil-producing olives in Beit-El [Bethel] and white earth in Tur Malka." While evidence for Deborah's wealth is not explicit in the text of Judges, if Deborah were indeed an eminently successful businesswoman in an era when the Israelite world of business, finance and entrepreneurship were dominated by men, her success may have propelled her to unusual heights of recognition, respect—and perhaps high office. Of course, her call by God to prophethood would have been completely independent of her wealth, if wealthy she was. Her exact status as a woman of little or great means may be yet another example of details lost amid the mists of history.

FIRST PREDICTION: THE HAZOR VICTORY

As mentioned earlier, the judges were, for the most part, military leaders who were required to marshall the Israelite forces against their enemies within and outside of Canaan. The fact that Deborah was a woman did not diminish the respect the Israelites had for her—or the support they gave to her—as their military leader. But the story of Deborah's military success is a tad more involved. While Deborah was the final authority who determined when and if Israel should commit its troops to battle, she herself was not a trained military tactician. Perhaps this is not dissimilar to the United States, whose President may choose to commit troops but who would not lead his troops into battle himself. Upon receiving a revelation from God, Deborah responded promptly:

> One day she sent for Barak, son of Abinoam from the city of Kedesh in Naphtali and said to him, "The Lord, the God of Israel, has given you this command: 'Take ten thousand men from the tribes of Naphtali and Zebulun and lead them to Mount Tabor. I will bring Sisera, the commander of Jabin's army, to fight you at the Kishon River. He will

> have his chariots and soldiers, but I will give you victory over him.'"
> (Judges 4:6-7)

During Deborah's time, Hazor was a powerful Canaanite city-state northwest of the Sea of Galilee. The fact that it was able to forge iron weapons and vehicles (unlike the Israelites, who were not yet schooled in ironworks) made Hazor that much more formidable. The general of the Hazor army was Sisera, a shrewd commander who was allegiant to the king of Hazor, called the "Jabin." Deborah's call to Barak to lead the Israelites against Hazor was clearly an executive decision made by a commander whose authority was unquestioned. But embedded within this order was a prophecy: that the Israelites would emerge victorious against a foe of great strength.

While Barak respectfully accepted the commission entrusted to him by Deborah, the two of them played something of a "cat-and-mouse" game before the troops were amassed. Barak accepted his commission conditionally:

> Then Barak replied, "I will go if you go with me, but if you don't go with me, I won't go either." (Judges 4:8)

In *Every Woman in the Bible*, Sue and Larry Richards see this condition as a positive view of Deborah through the eyes of Barak. "This reaction suggests how much credibility Deborah had as God's spokesperson and as Israel's leader. Barak felt inadequate; he was willing to fight only if Deborah was present at the battle...Barak viewed Deborah as a talisman, a symbol of the Divine Presence with His people." Perhaps these were exactly Barak's sentiments or perhaps not. It may have been equally true that Barak did not want to accept responsibility if the Israelite forces were unsuccessful—and thought that the presence of Deborah would provide him with a second scapegoat to bear the shame of failure. We will, of course, never really know Barak's deepest motivations.

SECOND PREDICTION: SISERA GOES TO JAEL

Nevertheless, Deborah accepted Barak's condition, but not without "upping the ante," so to speak, with yet another observation and prediction:

> She answered, "All right, I will go with you, but you won't get any credit for the victory, because the Lord will hand Sisera over to a woman." (Judges 4:9)

Deborah accompanied Barak and the Israelite army to Mount Tabor, from which vantage point the Israelites attacked Sisera's Hazor troops. It was at this time that Deborah's first prophecy of Israelite victory was realized:

> When Barak attacked with his army, the Lord threw Sisera into confusion together with all his chariots and men. Sisera got down from his chariot and fled on foot. Barak pursued the chariots and the army to Harosheth-of-the-Gentiles, and Sisera's whole army was killed. Not a man was left. (Judges 4:15-16)

This episode is not complete without a "sidebar" addition to the story that describes the accuracy of Deborah's second prediction that *the Lord will hand Sisera over to a woman.* Not far from the battlefield at Mount Tabor in Kedesh lived a Midianite (also known as Kenite) family—Heber and his wife Jael. Although Heber was a descendant of Moses' Midianite father-in-law Jethro, Heber was allegiant to the Jabin of Hazor rather than to the Israelites. When Sisera fled on foot from the battlefield, he found himself in the camp of Heber and Jael, whom he recognized as allies. But fortune did not smile on Sisera when he arrived there:

> *Sisera ran away to the tent of Jael, the wife of Heber the Kenite, because King Jabin of Hazor was at peace with Heber's family. Jael went out to meet Sisera and said to him, "Come in, Sir; come into my tent. Don't be afraid." So he went in, and she hid him behind a curtain. He said to her, "Please give me a drink of water; I'm thirsty." She opened a leather bag of milk, gave him a drink, and hid him again. Then he told her, "Stand at the door of the tent, and if anyone comes and asks you if anyone is here, say no."*
>
> *Sisera was so tired that he fell sound asleep. Then Jael took a hammer and a tent peg, quietly went up to him, and killed him by driving the peg right through the side of his head and into the ground. When Barak came looking for Sisera, Jael went out to meet him and said to him, "Come here! I'll show you the man you're looking for. So he went in with her, and there was Sisera on the ground, dead, with the tent peg through his head. (Judges 4:17-22)*

With the death of Sisera at the hands of Jael and the defeat of his army by Barak's forces, the Hazor oppression of the

Israelites ended—and Deborah's second prophecy came to fruition.

THE SONG OF DEBORAH AND BARAK

The final Scriptural passages that celebrate the extraordinary judgeship of Deborah are found in Chapter 5 of Judges, the entirety of which is a song of praise written by Deborah and sung by Deborah and Barak to commemorate God's benignity and to acknowledge everyone who contributed to the remarkable defeat of the forces of Hazor:

Praise the Lord! The Israelites were determined to fight; the people gladly volunteered.

Listen, you kings! Pay attention, you rulers!

I will sing and play music to Israel's God, the Lord.

Lord, when you left the mountains of Seir, when you came out of the region of Edom, the earth shook, and rain fell from the sky.

Yes, water poured down from the clouds.

The mountains quaked before the Lord of Sinai, before the Lord, the God of Israel.

In the days of Shamgar son of Anath, in the days of Jael, caravans no longer went through the land, and travelers used the back roads.

The towns of Israel stood abandoned, Deborah; they stood empty until you came, came like a mother for Israel.

Then there was war in the land when the Israelites chose new gods.

Of the forty thousand men in Israel, did anyone carry shield or spear?

My heart is with the commanders of Israel, with the people who gladly volunteered. Praise the Lord!

Tell of it, you that ride on white donkeys, sitting on saddles, and you that must walk wherever you go.

Listen! The noisy crowds around the wells are telling of the Lord's victories, the victories of Israel's people!

Then the Lord's people marched down from their cities.

Lead on, Deborah, lead on! Lead on! Sing a song! Lead on!

Forward, Barak son of Abinoam, lead your captives away!

Then the faithful ones came down to their leaders; the Lord's people came to him ready to fight.

They came from Ephraim into the valley, behind the tribe of Benjamin and its people.

The commanders came down from Machir, the officers down from Zebulun.

The leaders of Issachar came with Deborah; yes, Issachar came and Barak too, and they followed him into the valley.

But the tribe of Reuben was divided; they could not decide to come.

Why did they stay behind with the sheep? To listen to shepherds calling the flocks?

Yes, the tribe of Reuben was divided; they could not decide to come.

The tribe of Gad stayed east of the Jordan, and the tribe of Dan remained by the ships.

The tribe of Asher stayed by the seacoast; they remained along the shore.

But the people of Zebulun and Naphtali risked their lives on the battlefield.

At Taanach, by the stream of Megiddo, the kings came and fought;

the kings of Canaan fought, but they took no silver away.

The stars fought from the sky; as they moved across the sky, they fought against Sisera.

A flood in the Kishon swept them away—the onrushing Kishon River.

I shall march, march on, with strength!

Then the horses came galloping on, stamping the ground with their hoofs.

"Put a curse on Meroz," says the angel of the Lord, "a curse, a curse on those who live there.

They did not come to help the Lord, come as soldiers to fight for Him."

The most fortunate of women is Jael, the wife of Heber the Kenite—the most fortunate of women who live in tents.

Sisera asked for water, but she gave him milk; she brought him cream in a beautiful bowl.

She took a tent peg in one hand, a workman's hammer in the other;

she struck Sisera and crushed his skull; she pierced him through the head.

He sank to his knees, fell down and lay still at her feet.

At her feet he sank to his knees and fell; he fell to the ground, dead.

Sisera's mother looked out of the window; she gazed from behind the lattice.

"Why is his chariot so late in coming?" she asked. "Why are his horses so slow to return?"

Her wisest ladies answered her, and she told herself over and over,

"They are only finding things to capture and divide, a girl or two for every soldier, rich cloth for Sisera, embroidered, embroidered pieces for the neck of the queen."

So may all Your enemies die like that, O Lord, but may Your friends shine like the rising sun. (Judges 5:1-31)

This lengthy song brings the story of the judgeship and prophetic ministry of Deborah to its conclusion. This "Song of Deborah and Barak" offers words of praise to everyone who contributed to the defeat of Hazor, beginning with God and extending to Deborah and Barak, to the Israelite commanders and officers, to the volunteer combatants from the participating tribes—and finally to Jael, the wife of Heber the Kenite. Its closing verse records that Deborah's victory ushered in an unprecedented forty years of peace.

Although this chapter has been written to discuss Deborah, it would be unfair not to extend an acknowledgment to Jael as well. As mentioned earlier, in ancient Israelite society the women's responsibilities were invariably confined to domestic chores and the management of the household, while the men attended to matters of politics, economics and religion. Jael stands out as an independent, free-thinking woman who transcended the usual limitations placed on women. She subverted her husband Heber's tribal alliance with the Jabin of Hazor—with which she disagreed—and took matters into her own hands, to the advantage of Israel. Scripture doesn't record her husband's reaction to her behavior toward Sisera, but she should be commended for the courage and decisiveness of her actions.

Back now to Deborah. While different individuals may evaluate the administrations of each of the judges and rate or rank them in relation to one another, The Theology of Work Project, Inc., an international non-profit organization devoted to Christian Studies, reserved its highest accolades for Deborah, when it concluded, "The best of the judges is Deborah. The people recognize her wisdom and come to her for counsel and conflict resolution. The military hierarchy recognizes her as supreme commander and in fact will only go to war on her personal command. Her governance is so good that 'the land had rest for forty years,' a rare occurrence at any point in Israel's history."

QUESTIONS FOR REVIEW

1. What was unique about Deborah's responsibilities in the era in which she lived?

2. What prediction did Deborah make that can be used to cement her status as a prophetess?

3. Was Barak's insistence that Deborah accompany the Israelite troops into battle a sign of confidence or one of fear?

4. What was Deborah's second prediction? Was it accurate?

5. Is the "Song of Deborah and Barak" another example of her prophetic contributions? How?

Chapter Six
HANNAH

*H*annah is yet another inspirational woman who is viewed as a prophetess—not by designation in the Hebrew Scriptures—but through the insights and commentaries of the authors of the *Talmud*. Her story—and the example of faith, patience and forbearance that she offered—begins the First Book of Samuel, circa eleventh century BCE. Hannah's son Samuel served as the major transitional figure between the Age of Judges and the establishment of the monarchy in Israel in 1030 BCE.

It should be noted at the outset that there were several perhaps less-than-well-known customs that existed in Israel at the time Hannah lived. One of these was the importance of having a male heir to inherit property and to extend the family lineage. Tamar Kadari, in her article "Hannah: Midrash and Aggadah," explained, "The Midrash rules that if a couple has been married for ten years without having any children, the husband is obligated to take another (or additional) wife, in order to fulfill the commandment to be fruitful and multiply (M Yevamot 6:6)" (Please note that the assumption here is that the inability to procreate was the fault of the wife and not the husband!) It was in this very situation that Hannah found herself. After ten years of marriage without the blessing of children, Elkanah took a second wife, Peninnah, with whom he had five children. Elkanah loved Hannah deeply, a devotion that was not lost on Peninnah, who realized she would never be better than second place in Elkanah's heart.

Elkanah, who was descended from the tribe of Ephraim and who lived with his family in the town of Ramah, was a reverent and observant follower of the Lord:

> *Every year Elkanah went from Ramah to worship and offer sacrifices to the Lord Almighty at Shiloh, where Hophni and Phinehas, the two sons of Eli, were priests of the Lord. Each time Elkanah offered his sacrifice, he would give one share of the meat to Peninnah and one share to each of her children.*
>
> *And to Hannah, however, he would give a special share because he loved her very much even though the Lord had kept her from having children.* (1 Samuel 1:2-5)

However, the family's annual pilgrimages to Shiloh were punctuated with discord due to the incessant mockery of Peninnah toward the childless Hannah:

> *Peninnah, her [Hannah's] rival, would torment and humiliate her because the Lord had kept her childless. This went on year after year;*

whenever they went to the house of the Lord, Peninnah would upset Hannah so much that she would cry and refuse to eat anything. Her husband Elkanah would ask her, "Hannah, why are you crying? Why won't you eat? Why are you always so sad? Don't I mean more to you than ten sons?" (1 Samuel 1:6-78)

Elkanah was clearly aware that Hannah was grieving over her inability to conceive, but it isn't known if he was aware of the extent and depth of Peninnah's insults and mockery.

ONGOING ANGUISH

The house of the Lord at Shiloh was supervised and maintained by the priest Eli, who was assisted by his two sons Hophni and Phinehas. During one of the family's sojourns to Shiloh, Hannah became greatly agitated. It's unclear if her upsetment was a direct result of Peninnah's barbs (the Bible doesn't specify), but Hannah found herself in a deeply troubled emotional state in the temple precincts:

> *She was deeply distressed, and she cried bitterly as she prayed to the Lord.*
>
> *Meanwhile, Eli the priest was sitting in his place by the door. Hannah made a solemn promise: "Lord Almighty, look at Your servant! See my trouble and remember me! Don't forget me! If You give me a son, I promise that I will dedicate him to You for his whole life and that he will never have his hair cut* [a sign of dedication to the Lord]*."* (1 Samuel 1:9-11)

It was the convention at this time to pray aloud in the temple, whereas today we are more inclined to offer our prayers and petitions silently and privately. But since Hannah, in her state of despondency, chose not to follow this prevailing custom, she caught the suspicious eye of Eli:

> *Hannah continued to pray to the Lord for a long time, and Eli watched her lips.*
>
> *She was praying silently; her lips were moving, but she made no sound. So Eli thought she was drunk, and he said to her, "Stop making a drunken show of yourself! Stop your drinking and sober up!" (1 Samuel 1:12-14)*

Already in great distress, the last thing Hannah needed was to be accused of public drunkenness—and possible desecration—on the grounds of the temple or to incur the wrath of the eminent and respected high priest Eli. So she promptly responded:

> *No, I'm not drunk, sir...I haven't been drinking! I am desperate, and I have been praying, pouring out my troubles to the Lord. Don't think I am a worthless woman. I have been praying like this because I'm so miserable. (1 Samuel 1:15-16)*

Scripture does not record a follow-up conversation between Hannah and Eli where Hannah may have unburdened herself to the high priest and convinced him of her heartfelt desire to give birth. Whatever may have been said between them remains a mystery, but it is clear that Eli realized the error of his first opinion of Hannah, when he said:

> *Go in peace...and may the God of Israel give you what you have asked Him for. (1 Samuel 1:17)*

It seems that the words of Eli the high priest, which were considered to be prophetic, gave support and encouragement that transformed Hannah, whose attitude instantly brightened. And beyond that, Hannah's simple and fervent prayer may have been instrumental in reversing her fortunes, for upon her return to Ramah, she promptly became pregnant, and gave birth to her son Samuel, whose name means "asked of the Lord." Samuel was a Nazirite—one who was consecrated to the Lord in perpetuity, and the sign of this commitment was that his hair would never be cut. (The judge Samson was also a Nazirite, whose great physical strength from God emanated from his unshorn locks, until he was betrayed by his wife Delilah.)

THE PRAYER/PSALM/ODE OF HANNAH

Hannah kept Samuel at home with her until he had been weaned, and then she sought to fulfill the promise she had made to God on her last trip to Shiloh. So Hannah brought Samuel to Eli and offered him to Eli to begin his training for the priesthood. As they worshipped the Lord at Shiloh, Hannah prayed with these words:

> *The Lord has filled my heart with joy; how happy I am because of what He has done!*

I laugh at my enemies; how joyful I am because God has helped me!

No one is holy like the Lord; there is none like Him, no protector like our God.

Stop your loud boasting; silence your proud words.

For the Lord is a God Who knows, and He judges all that people do.

The bows of strong soldiers are broken, but the weak grow strong.

The people who once were well fed now hire themselves out to get food, but the hungry are hungry no more.

The childless wife has borne seven children, but the mother of many is left with none.

The Lord kills and restores to life; He sends people to the world of the dead and brings them back again.

He makes some men poor and others rich; he humbles some and makes others great.

He lifts the poor from the dust and raises the needy from their misery.

He makes them companions of princes and puts them in places of honor.

The foundations of the earth belong to the Lord; on them He has built the world.

He protects the lives of His faithful people, but the wicked disappear in darkness; a man does not triumph by his own strength.

The Lord's enemies will be destroyed; He will thunder against them from heaven.

The Lord will judge the whole world; He will give power to His king, He will make His chosen king victorious. (1 Samuel 2:1-10)

It is these spoken words of Hannah that have led many rabbis to consider Hannah to be a prophet, and this prayer, in different quarters, has been called either "Hannah's Prayer", or "Hannah's Psalm of Thanksgiving," or "Ode of the Prophetess Hannah."

SIGNIFICANCE OF THE HORN

While this book has used the *Good News Bible* as its primary Scriptural source, it is certainly a well-known fact that the Bible has been translated many times over as our own vocabulary and patterns of speech have likewise adapted to changing times and circumstances. Therefore, it is important to note that it is in another translation of the First Book of Samuel—in this case the *New American Bible* (1970), among others—that the wording of Hannah's Prayer is slightly different. And that difference becomes important. Where the *Good News Bible* translates a portion of 1 Samuel 2:1 as "The Lord has filled my heart with joy; how happy I am because of what He has done...", the *New American Bible* offers, "My heart exults in the Lord, my horn is exalted in my God..." it is the use of the word "horn" that takes on special significance.

Dr. Wilda C. Gafney's *Daughters of Miriam: Women Prophets in Ancient Israel* offers an explanation. "The rabbis understood Hannah to have been a prophet because of her song in 1 Samuel 2. Philo [the 2nd century BCE Greek philosopher] also recognizes Hannah as a prophet. The essential verse for the rabbis is 1 Samuel 1:1...Hannah's reference to her "horn" leads to the understanding that she prophesied the rise of the Davidic dynasty. David and Solomon are anointed with a horn of oil in 1 Samuel 16:3 and 26:13 and 1 Kings 1:39, while Saul and Jehu are anointed with another type of vessel. Hannah's knowledge of God's plans for the Davidic dynasty and her proclamation of those plans makes her a prophet in the eyes of the rabbis."

Welsh Presbyterian minister Matthew Henry, in his *Complete Bible Commentary* (1706), thought that this prophecy of Hannah in 1 Samuel 2 was even more far-reaching than the upcoming kingships of David and Solomon, when he suggested, "We have reason to think that this prophecy looks further, to the kingdom of Christ, and the administration of that kingdom of grace, of which she [Hannah] now comes to speak, having spoken so largely of the kingdom of providence. And here is the first time that we meet the name Messiah, or His Anointed. The ancient expositors, both Jewish and Christian, make it to look beyond David, to the Son of David."

While this may seem like rather flimsy evidence on which to make an exalted claim of prophethood, this is not the only justification. Protopresbyter George Papavarnavas of the Antiochian Archdiocese of the Greek Orthodox Church found another piece of evidence to call Hannah a prophetess when he compared her altercation with Eli with a similar occurrence in the New Testament: "When the Apostles received the Holy Spirit on the day of Pentecost, whoever saw them or heard them speak, passed them off for drunks. The Prophetess Hannah, when she opened her heart to God inside the Temple, must have been 'filled with the Holy Spirit,' which is why Eli passed her off as a drunk." For Papavarnavas, this moment of "divine inspiration" is sufficient to view Hannah as an authentic spokesperson for God.

One final note about the Prayer of Hannah: it is often viewed as a parallel text to the "Magnificat" of Mary in the New Testament, prayed by Mary when she visited her cousin Elizabeth shortly after the Annunciation of the Angel Gabriel. Both prayers reflect similar themes of praise and gratitude. As Mary proclaimed, so like Hannah did generations earlier:

> *My heart praises the Lord; my soul is glad because of God my Savior, For He has remembered me, His lowly servant!*
>
> *From now on all people will call me happy, because of the great things the Mighty God has done for me.*
>
> *His name is holy; from one generation to another He has shown mercy To those who honor Him.*
>
> *He has stretched out His mighty arm and scattered the proud with all their plans.*
>
> *He has brought down mighty kings from their thrones, and lifted up the lowly.*
>
> *He has filled the hungry with good things, and sent the rich away with empty hands.*
>
> *He has kept the promise He made to our ancestors, and has come to the help of His servant Israel.*
>
> *He has remembered to show mercy to Abraham and to all his descendants forever. (Luke 1:46-56)*

The early life of Hannah was dominated by one desire—to bear a son. Her inability to do so was a tremendous source of embarrassment, self-doubt and consternation to her—leading to her commitment to turn her beloved son back to the service of God in the event that she did bear one. But Hannah's frustration never yielded either to anger or apostasy. She simply prayed all the harder. And when she found herself on the receiving end of Peninnah's insults, she never got angry or responded in kind. And when her prayers were answered, Hannah was good to her word and delivered what she promised—a Nazirite boy to serve God as a priest. Was Hannah a prophetess—as we understand the word? Scripture doesn't call her one, but the ancient rabbis who compiled the Talmud did. They believe she was able to predict the future—perhaps as far away as a millenium—above and beyond the exemplary life of prayer, gentleness and faith that sustained her. So whether Hannah was a prophetess or not, she still resonates with us as a perfect example of a life well lived.

QUESTIONS FOR REVIEW

1. Why did Elkanah find it imperative to take a second wife?

2. What was the nature of the relationship between Peninnah and Hannah?

3. Why did the high priest Eli accuse Hannah of public drunkenness?

4. What is a Nazirite? Why is Samuel a Nazirite?

5. Why have the words in Hannah's Prayer led some theologians to consider Hannah to be an authentic prophetess?

6. What similarities exist between "Hannah's Prayer" and the "Magnificat" of Mary?

Chapter Seven
ABIGAIL

When the movie version of the hit Broadway play "Godspell" was turned into a movie, the opening musical number was changed. Instead of the philosophical "Tower of Babble," John the Baptist, sounding his shofar (ram's horn), called each of the Apostles to follow Jesus as He began His public ministry. John "appeared" to different individuals from various walks of life—cab driver, ballerina, delivery man, actress, etc.—sending a clear message that God might choose *anyone*, regardless of gender, career or social status—to serve Him.

It's common knowledge that throughout both the Old and New Testaments, those who have been called to serve as either prophets or disciples have been drawn from the ranks of farmers, fishermen, doctors, shepherds, judges and domestics. Is it possible that, in the case of Abigail, God may have chosen an abused wife as an instrument of His will? For when we read the saga of Abigail as recorded in the First Book of Samuel, we're led to believe that may have—tragically—been the case. Abuse, of course, is not confined to physical brutality. It can be verbal, emotional, financial—or even sexual. While 1 Samuel may be short on details, however, it is not an unreasonable conclusion to draw circumstantially that abuse was probably present.

To understand why the rabbis who compiled the *Talmud* listed Abigail on its roster of prophetesses, it's necessary to offer a bit of background information. Abigail lived during the reign of Saul, the first king of Israel. Saul's reign began well enough, as he spearheaded several decisive military victories against other Canaanite tribes who were hoping to expand their influence, but deteriorated quickly when Saul failed to follow the Lord's specific instructions in battling an enemy known as the Amalekites. God required that Saul complete a *herem* (ban)—a total annihilation of the tribe—but Saul failed to do this, claiming that his intention was to honor God in a different way. This may or may not have been Saul's real intention, but we will probably never know his true motivation.

In any event, God's displeasure with Saul led the Lord to send the prophet Samuel to tell Saul that God was preparing to remove him as king, causing Saul to lapse into a state of depression. Samuel then secretly anointed David of Bethlehem, the youngest son of Jesse, to serve as the next king. Ironically, David, a musician, was then called to the court of Saul to use music—his skills on the harp—to soothe the troubled king. Although Saul took a liking to young David (completely unaware that he had been anointed by Samuel to succeed him as king), his affection turned to jealousy when David defeated the Philistine giant Goliath in "mano-a-mano combat"—thereby earning recognition and accolades that eclipsed those of the king. From this point on, the relationship between Saul and David soured completely. While David never expressed the slightest disloyalty to King Saul either in word or deed, Saul's desire to destroy David became obsessive, bordering on paranoia. Saul attempted to kill David on a number of occasions, despite assurances from his own son Jonathan and other military leaders that David's loyalty was beyond reproach. At the time when David first encountered Abigail, he and his supporters were "on the run" from Saul's soldiers—virtual outlaws in a country where they had done no wrong.

A MATCH NOT MADE IN HEAVEN

Finally, this brings us to Abigail. Nothing is recorded in Scripture of her parentage, place of birth or background, but she is held in very high regard as a woman of unsurpassed beauty coupled with great intelligence, loyalty and a self-effacing flair for diplomacy. In many ways she seems to be the complete opposite of her husband Nabal, an incredibly rich yet boorish, cruel man who was prone to bouts of drunkenness.

> *There was a man of the clan of Caleb named Nabal, who was from the town of Maon, and who owned land near the town of Carmel. He was a very rich man, the owner of three thousand sheep and one thousand goats. His wife Abigail was beautiful and intelligent, but he was a mean, bad-tempered man. (1 Samuel 25:2-3)*

Marg Mowczko of Macquarie University in Sydney, Australia described Nabal's name as "a Hebrew word that means 'foolish' or 'senseless.' As an adjective, *nabal* is sometimes used [to describe] people who have no perception of ethical or religious claims. It's an apt name for Abigail's husband who typifies such behavior."

David and his supporters, approximately 600 of them, found themselves in the vicinity of Nabal's property, and they took it upon themselves to offer protection to the shepherds employed by Nabal and to the flocks entrusted to their care. It clearly would have been well within their capabilities to attack the shepherds and plunder their sheep if they so wished, but that was not their intent. Rather, David sent a party of ten of his followers to deliver a message to Nabal, who was shearing his sheep in Carmel.

> *He instructed them to say to Nabal: "David sends you greetings, my friend, with his best wishes for you, your family and all that is yours.*
>
> *He heard that you were shearing your sheep and he wants you to know that your shepherds have been with us and we did not harm them. Nothing that belonged to them was stolen...Just ask them and they will tell you. We have come on a feast day, and David asks you to receive us kindly. Please give what you can to us your servants and to your dear friend David." (1 Samuel 25:6-8)*

The messengers' comment that "we have come on a feast day" is rather significant. In her 2012 text *A Woman God Can Use*, Dr. Alice Mathews of the Gordon-Conwell Theological Seminary pointed out, '...the story...opens during the time of year when

Nabal's three thousand sheep were being shorn. That is a lot of sheep, a lot of shearers, and a lot of work for everyone concerned. Sheepshearing season in Nabal's day was also a festive time. It was customary for the sheep owner to provide a feast when the job was done. At that feast he would give gifts to everyone who had helped in any way during the year. This was a token of thanks to God and a gesture of goodwill to his neighbors. When David sent his young men to collect what was due to them for the protection they had provided Nabal's shepherds during the year, they had every reason to expect Nabal to be generous...First, he should have responded generously to them for the help they had given his shepherds. Second...custom required him to be polite to them even if David had been a deadly enemy. Not only did wicked, surly, mean Nabal refuse to give anything when he should have given freely, but he also scorned David's character in front of his men."

Despite King Saul's unreasonable jealousy of David and the state of tension that existed between them, it was not known to Saul or to the general public that Samuel had already anointed David to serve as the next king of Israel. Neither had David said or done anything to suggest he was hoping to usurp the throne. Rather, David had been consistently loyal to Saul, although Saul's envy was preventing him from seeing this. In any event, David was very well-known throughout Israel because of his successful military campaigns in support of King Saul, so Nabal's response to David's messengers was unexpected and confusing.

> *David's men delivered this message in David's name. Then they waited there, and Nabal finally answered, "David? Who is he? I've never heard of him! The country is full of runaway slaves nowadays! I'm not going to take my bread and water, and the animals I have butchered for my sheep shearers, and give them to people who come from I don't know where!" (1 Samuel 25:10-11)*

When David's messengers returned to him with Nabal's response, David was quite incensed. Between being insulted as a "runaway slave" and experiencing both Nabal's ingratitude and greed, David was prepared to exact a very violent, very bloody vengeance. Gathering his sword and instructing his men to do likewise, David was preparing to attack with 400 of his men. However, David was unaware of the goings-on at Nabal's own residence.

> *One of Nabal's servants said to Nabal's wife Abigail, "Have you heard?*
>
> *David sent some messengers from the wilderness with greetings for our master, but he insulted them. Yet, they were very good to us; they never bothered us, and all the time we were with them in the fields, nothing that belonged to us was stolen. They protected us day and night the whole time we were with them looking after our flocks. Please think this over and decide what to do. This could be disastrous for our master and all his family. He is so mean that he won't listen to anybody!" (1 Samuel 14-17)*

A RISKY INTERVENTION

The events that followed this revelation to Abigail set the stage for her not only to showcase her decisiveness, diplomacy and bravery, but also to provide the necessary evidence for the rabbis of the *Talmud* to designate her as a prophetess. First, her decisiveness:

> *Abigail quickly gathered two hundred loaves of bread, two leather bags full of wine, five roasted sheep, two bushels of roasted grain, a hundred bunches of raisins, and two hundred cakes of dried figs, and loaded them on donkeys.*
>
> *Then she said to the servants, "You go on ahead and I will follow you." But she said nothing to her husband. (1 Samuel 25:18-19)*

Abigail took quick action to reverse what she suspected could turn into an upcoming bloodbath. But there was no guarantee that her gathering of supplies to feed David and his men would necessarily prevent a catastrophe. That is where her sense of diplomacy came into play, as she absorbed the blame for her husband's boorishness while at the same time treating David with the utmost respect and deference:

> *She was riding her donkey around a bend on a hillside when suddenly she met David and his men coming toward her. David had been thinking, "Why did I ever protect that fellow's property out here in the wilderness?...This is how he pays me back for the help I gave him! May God strike me dead if I don't kill every last one of those men before morning!"*

> *When Abigail saw David, she quickly dismounted and threw herself on the ground at David's feet, and said to him, "Please, sir, listen to me! Let me take the blame. Please don't pay any attention to Nabal, that good-for-nothing! He is exactly what his name means—a fool! I wasn't there when your servants arrived, sir. It is the Lord Who has kept you from taking revenge and killing your enemies...Please, sir, accept this present I have brought you, and give it to your men." (1 Samuel 25:23-27)*

ABIGAIL'S PROPHECY

When Abigail met David, it wasn't only her gesture of generosity and support that touched David and encouraged him to reverse his plans of revenge and annihilation. He could not help but notice—nor did the rabbis who compose the *Talmud*—that Abigail was clearly inspired by God as one of His prophetesses went she went on to say:

> The Lord will make you king, and your descendants also, because you are fighting His battles; and no evil will happen to you as long as you live. If anyone should attack you and try to kill you, the Lord your God will keep you safe, as a man guards a precious treasure. As for your enemies, however, He will throw them away, as a man hurls stones with his sling. And when the Lord has done all the good things He has promised you and has made you king of Israel, then you will not have to feel regret or remorse, sir, for having killed without cause or for having taken your own revenge." (1 Samuel 25:28-31)

Certainly David was aware that Abigail would have no way of knowing that Samuel had already anointed him as the next king of Israel. So he responded to her with acceptance and appreciation:

> David said to her, "Praise the Lord, the God of Israel, who sent you today to meet me! Thank God for your good sense and for what you have done today in keeping me from the crime of murder and from taking my own revenge. The Lord has kept me from harming you. But I swear by the living God of Israel that if you had not hurried to meet me, all of Nabal's men would have been dead by morning!" Then David accepted what she had brought him and said to her, "Go back home and don't worry. I will do what you want." (1 Samuel 25:32-35)

It's possible that Abigail's great bravery could get lost "in the shuffle" in the drama of the moment. Marg Mowczko pointed out how Abigail's courage was exhibited on two different fronts. The first front was in her encounter with David and his men. "Abigail was not just intelligent and beautiful, she was also brave. It would have been no mean feat to confront David and four hundred of his men who had been dishonored and were intent on revenge with their swords at the ready. Yet Abigail approached David and, with great diplomacy, humbly offered him a 'peace offering.'"

Abigail had chosen not to inform Nabal of her plans to reverse his decision and provide food (and apologies) to David and his supporters.(Nabal had been feasting and was quite drunk when his servant had approached Abigail). But as Mowczko also points out, "Abigail was also brave considering that her actions would be found out by her husband, and then she would have to face his violent temper." Yet, her confession to Nabal turned out quite differently.

> ...*After he had sobered up, she told him everything. He suffered a stroke and was completely paralyzed. Some ten days later the Lord struck Nabal and he died.* (1 Samuel 25:37-38)

Abigail's story could end here—and she would have established herself as a prophetess of great beauty, intelligence, courage and cunning—but the saga goes on a little further.

> *When David heard that Nabal had died, he said, "Praise the Lord! He has taken revenge on Nabal for insulting me and has kept me His servant from doing wrong. The Lord has punished Nabal for his evil." Then David sent a proposal of marriage to Abigail...Abigail bowed down to the ground and said, "I am his servant, ready to wash the feet of his servants."...Accompanied by her five maids, she went with David's servants and became his wife.* (1 Samuel 25:39, 41-42)

Abigail became the third wife of David, following Michal and Ahinoam. With David she had a son named Chileab, but the Bible then offers no more information about her later life.

Rabbi Peter Tarlow of Texas A & M University offered perhaps the clearest description of Abigail and the virtues she displayed. "Abigail, like the other female prophetesses, was a strong woman. Her life teaches us that no matter what life deals to us, if we have faith in ourselves and in God, we can turn crises into blessings and difficulties into opportunities. When we study her life we see that, just as in the case of other Biblical personages, her life was filled...with unexpected twists and turns...Despite, or perhaps because of, the undulations in her life the prophetess Abigail serves as a role model for all of us...Abigail's life reminds us that if we are both strong of faith and of character we can control the direction of our lives. No matter what might have been the circumstances of her life, she found a way to shape its direction. Abigail was, at heart, an optimist, and her life reminds us of the words of Theodore Herzl: 'if you will it, it is no dream!'"

QUESTIONS FOR REVIEW

1. How would you describe the personal qualities that both Abigail and Nabal brought to their marriage?

2. Why was David in a position to offer protection to the sheep and shepherds of Nabal?

3. What was Nabal expected to give David and his men? Why did Nabal refuse to do this?

4. In what way(s) did Nabal insult David?

5. What was David's response to the insult he received from Nabal?

6. How did Abigail show (1) good judgment, (2) diplomacy and (3) bravery in her response to this crisis?

7. What did Abigail say that led the rabbis to consider her to be an authentic prophetess?

8. What were the reasons that David was grateful to Abigail?

Chapter Eight
"THE PROPHETESS"

*I*n the second chapter of this book, I pointed out that the women discussed herein as prophetesses would include members of the following groups: those who are referred to as prophetesses in the Old Testament, those whose actions fall within the parameters of the definition of prophet (even if they are not called so by name), and those who are considered prophetesses by the esteemed rabbis who composed and compiled the *Talmud*. The subject of this chapter—"The Prophetess"—has been the topic of much discussion and debate throughout the ages primarily due to the fact that she has remained nameless. The 8th century BCE prophet Isaiah of Jerusalem reported:

> Some time later my wife became pregnant. When our son was born, the Lord said to me, "Name him Quick-Loot-Fast-Plunder. Before the boy is old enough to say 'Mamma' and 'Daddy,' all the wealth of Damascus

> *and all the loot of Samaria will be carried off by the king of Assyria."* (Isaiah 8:3-4)

> *Then I went to the prophetess and she conceived and bore a son. The Lord said to me: "Name him Maher-shalal-hash-baz, for before the child knows how to call his father or mother by name, the wealth of Damascus and the spoil of Samaria shall be carried off by the king of Assyria."* (Isaiah 8:3-4)

It is fascinating to compare translations of the Bible. The first translation above comes from the *Good News Bible: Today's English Version*, which I will use consistently throughout this text. The second translation of exactly the same quote from the Book of Isaiah comes from *The New American Bible* (1970), with the Imprimatur of Patrick Cardinal O'Boyle, the former Archbishop of Washington DC.

Please note the use of the phrase "my wife" (in the *Good News Bible*) as it is contrasted with the phrase "the prophetess" (in the *New American Bible*). The original Hebrew employs the word *neviah* to describe this woman—and *neviah* is invariably translated as "prophetess." Most contemporary translations of the Book of Isaiah employ the phrase "the prophetess," and it is generally assumed that the prophetess in question is, indeed, the wife of the prophet Isaiah of Jerusalem. The *Good News Bible* states this explicitly despite the fact that this phrase is really only an inference. So the status of this woman—the mother of Isaiah's son—raises a series of additional questions about her role in the prophetic ministry of ancient Israel. Is she called a prophetess in most translations of the Bible because she has displayed some of the attributes (as mentioned in chapter two) of prophethood—even if they are not further articulated or described in Scripture? Or is this a designation given to her simply to acknowledge her intimate relationship with an authentic prophet? Is her prophethood merely a refracted one?

Perhaps at this point it would be a good idea to step back and review some pertinent information about the prophet Isaiah. He was the son of Amoz, and worked in the royal court of Judah as a historiographer, a chronicler of historical records in the seventh and eighth centuries BCE during the reign of four of Judah's kings: Uzziah, Jotham, Ahaz and Hezekiah. He fathered two sons—Mahershalalhashbaz (meaning "quick loot, fast plunder") and Shearjashub (a name which means "a remnant shall return")—both of whose names, it is believed, have predictive meanings. Biblical scholars largely agree that the Book of Isaiah, which spans two and a half centuries of history, was probably written by two or three different authors, aptly designated Isaiah of Jerusalem, Second (or Deutero) Isaiah and Third (or Trito) Isaiah. Historically, it is only Isaiah of Jerusalem whose identity is verified.

GUILD PROPHET?

If we assume that "The Prophetess" is the wife of Isaiah, it doesn't really shed any additional information about her as a prophet in her own right. The pertinent details simply don't exist to either prove or disprove her prophetic ministry. As a result, opinions on both sides assert themselves. In a 2013 blog post, Dr. Claude Mariottini of the Northern Baptist Seminary offered, "Personally, I believe that Isaiah's wife was a prophet who exercised a prophetic ministry alongside her husband. According to Isaiah 8:16, Isaiah had a group of disciples who preserved his oracles.

> *You, my disciples, are to guard and preserve the messages that God has given me." (Isaiah 8:16)*

Thus, it is possible that Isaiah's wife was part of this prophetic guild and worked with him by giving symbolic names to their sons as visible evidence of the message Isaiah preached to King Ahaz." [The name *Shearjashub* predicted the return to Judah of a population that had been removed and enslaved, and *Maher-shalal-hash-baz* was a prophetic prediction made by Isaiah to King Ahaz that Damascus and Samaria were soon to be overrun by the forces of Assyria].

Dr. Mariottini included several additional observations to support his contention that The Prophetess was an authentic prophet in her own right. He wrote in the same blog, "A survey of the Hebrew Bible shows that the prophets never called their wives 'prophetesses.' The prophet Ezekiel was married, and when he spoke about his wife he said, 'My wife died.' (Ezekiel 24:18) Ezekiel never called his wife a neviah, a prophetess. The prophet Hosea was married to Gomer and when he spoke about his wife, he called her 'my wife', not 'the prophetess.' (Hosea 2:2) On the other hand, every time the word neviah is used in the Hebrew Bible, it refers to a Hebrew woman who exercises an authentic prophetic ministry. Deborah was a neviah and the wife of Lappidoth...Huldah was a neviah and the wife of Shallum...Miriam was a neviah...Noadiah was a neviah...The information provided by the texts where the word "neviah" appears clearly indicates that each woman was a neviah, not because she was married to a prophet, but because she exercised the prophetic ministry, because of a divine call, and because she had received the endowment of the Spirit."

Those who disagree argue that it is possible that The Prophetess was *not* the wife of Isaiah. The text of the Book of Isaiah never explicitly says that she is. Theologian Joseph Blenkinsopp of the University of Notre Dame wrote in his book *A History of Prophecy in Israel* (1983) that, "We are not told that this anonymous woman was Isaiah's wife...We therefore assume that she is, or is represented as being, an officially recognized member of the nabi class...perhaps also a member of the Jerusalem temple staff." Dr. Wilda C. Gafney of the Lutheran Theological Seminary agreed with this in her text *Daughters of Miriam: Women Prophets in Ancient Israel* (2008): "The female prophet with whom Isaiah conceives his son Maher-shalal-hash-baz is not named in the text, nor is she specifically identified as his woman/wife...It is ...possible that they were not married, since none of the traditional language invoking what has come to be called 'marriage' is employed." Nevertheless, Dr. Gafney goes on to say that, "The production of a child whose name is a portent of the future of Judah is a prophetic performance...depicting a joint prophetic undertaking by Isaiah and the Woman-Prophet. Given the mores of the time, the Deuteronomic language, and Isaiah's acceptance among temple and palace elite, it is likely that they were a conjugal couple."

The story of "The Prophetess" in Isaiah leaves many unanswered questions about both her prophetic role and her relationship to Isaiah. Nevertheless, it seems to be the consensus of most Biblical scholars that her designation as "The Prophetess" is far from honorific. We may not know much about her, but the knowledge we do possess permits us to include her among the ranks of those prophets who have richly contributed to salvation history.

QUESTIONS FOR REVIEW

1. What is the primary difficulty in viewing Isaiah of Jerusalem's wife as a prophetess?

2. What evidence has led Dr. Claude Marriottini to consider her to be an authentic prophet?

3. Why does Dr. Wilda C. Gafney agree with this conclusion?

Chapter Nine
HULDAH

*I*t has often been suggested that the accuracy of some historical records can be considered suspect because they have invariably been written by the "winners," who slant their chronicles to favor themselves as well as to disparage their victims and adversaries (the "losers"). Perhaps a similar criticism can be made about the composition of the Old Testament along the lines of gender. Is it possible that the Old Testament (or *Hebrew Scriptures*, if you prefer)—which we have historically believed to have been written primarily by men—has either deliberately or inadvertently omitted or diminished the contributions of many women whose words and ministries may have played a critical, albeit undocumented, role in Judaic history?

This would seem to be the case with the prophetess Huldah, who lived in the seventh century BCE during the reign of King Josiah of Judah. But Huldah's role in Judaic history cannot be discussed properly without a digression into Judaic politics and apostasy during the time period immediately preceding her.

HISTORICAL BACKGROUND

The ascendancy of King Rehoboam, Solomon's son, to the throne of Israel upon his father's death in 931 BCE became a watershed moment in the history of the Israelites. Solomon, despite being a recipient of the divine gift of wisdom, became more and more oppressive to his own subjects in the latter years of his reign. Heavy taxation and forced conscription alienated his people such that when Rehoboam was crowned king, the Israelite citizenry petitioned him for greater leniency. However, yielding to the counsel of some of his close comrades who told him that yielding to such a request would be construed as a sign of weakness, Rehoboam rejected the plea and promised even greater restrictions and deprivations. This short-sighted and insensitive decision proved disastrous—the proverbial "straw that broke the camel's back." Ten of the twelve tribes of Israel seceded, and the Israelites split into two separate nations—Israel, to the north, consisting of the ten apostate tribes, and Judah, to the south, composed of the two tribes (Benjamin and Judah) who remained loyal to Rehoboam and the Davidic throne.

Because this schism left both nations weaker and more vulnerable than they would have been had they remained united, the northern kingdom of Israel was conquered by Assyria approximately two hundred years later in 721 BCE. Many of its citizens were exiled far away to the north of Israel, where they eventually lost both their cultural identity and Yahwistic faith, eventually earning the dubious distinction of being called "the ten lost tribes of Israel." Rabbi Roy A. Rosenberg's 1990 *Concise Guide to Judaism: History, Practice, Faith* explained that "the Assyrians brought foreign peoples to settle the land. These mingled with the few Israelites who had not gone into exile and adopted the worship of Yahweh. They are referred to in Jewish circles as the Samaritans, after Samaria, the capital city of Israel." However, the changing population of Israel (a.k.a. Samaria) and the intermarriage of the remaining Israelites with immigrants from other parts of the Assyrian Empire ultimately led to a syncretic mixing of religious faith and practices, resulting in the introduction of other gods into worship practices. When these Israelites began to worship Canaanite deities such as the fertility god Baal —in some cases joining and in other cases replacing Yahweh— they were in direct violation of the first commandment given to them at Mount Sinai:

> *I am the Lord your God, who brought you out of Egypt where you were slaves. Worship no god but Me. (Exodus 20:2)*

The people of the southern kingdom of Judah witnessed with horror and revulsion the idolatry and polytheism that had corrupted Israel, and the chasm between these two nations of the Chosen People widened even further. However, the theological aberrations that had insidiously infected Israel were not confined to the northern kingdom; they inexorably crept southward into Judah. A series of Judahite (or Judean) kings permitted—and in some cases even encouraged—rejection of Yahweh and devotion to other deities.

Chapters 8 through 22 in the Second Book of Kings chronicle the eleven monarchs of Judah who ruled in the two centuries from the beginning of the reign of King Jehoram in 848 BCE to the beginning of the reign of King Josiah in 640 BCE. This time period in the history of Judah was characterized by tremendous political turmoil and by even greater idolatry and apostasy. Some Judean monarchs were downright abominable in their rejection of Yahweh—King Jehoram (848-841 BCE), King Ahaziah (841 BCE), Queen Athaliah (841-835 BCE), King Ahaz (736-716 BCE), King Manasseh (687-642 BCE) and King Amon (642-640 BCE). Others kings—Joash (835-796 BCE), Amaziah ((796-781 BCE) Uzziah (781-740 BCE) and Jotham (740-736 BCE)—were personally respectful of Yahweh but tepid; they did nothing to shut down the ongoing idolatrous practices of the people, even if they did not participate in these practices and rituals themselves.

The only king who was truly devoted to Yahweh, and relentless in his efforts to purge Judah of idolatry and wickedness, was King Hezekiah, who ruled from 716-687 BCE. David Mandel, in *Who's Who in the Hebrew Bible* (2014), listed Hezekiah's efforts to restore true devotion to Yahweh. "Hezekiah's first act as king was to re-open the gates of the Temple and to have them repaired. He asked the priests and Levites to purify the Temple...he...eradicated idolatry throughout the country...Hezekiah died loved and honored by his people and was succeeded by his son Manasseh."

Unfortunately, Hezekiah's herculean efforts to restore devotion to Yahweh and eradicate idolatry were short-lived. His son

Manasseh was as evil as Hezekiah was good—and subverted all of Hezekiah's efforts.

Rabbi Eli Kavon, in the *Jerusalem Post*, described this reversal in detail. "The difference between father and son could not have been more dramatic. Manasseh ruled Judah for 55 years...longer than any king of Judah. If we rely on the prophetic portions of the Bible alone, the portrait that is painted is of an evil man—a mass murderer and idol worshipper whose reign was so tainted it would later be the cause of the Babylonian destruction of Jerusalem and the Temple of Solomon in 586 BCE. Manasseh promoted idolatry throughout his kingdom, built pagan temples and even sacrificed one of his sons in the fires of Moloch [a Canaanite god] worship."

Manasseh was succeeded as king by his 22-year-old son Amon who, incidentally, was named after the Egyptian sun god, Amon-Ra—yet more evidence of idolatry. Amon reigned for only two years, continuing his father's idolatrous practices and leading his people further and further away from Yahweh. Several of his own officials, recognizing that Amon was leading his people down the wrong path, assassinated him. These officials, ironically, were then killed by the people of Judah, who then placed Amon's son Josiah on the throne. Josiah was 8 years old.

This chapter, as you know, is named for Huldah, but nary a word has yet been written about this prophetess. The reason for this is that her contributions to the people of Judah and their religious heritage cannot be discussed, much less appreciated, without placing them in their proper historical context. For the two hundred years preceding Josiah's ascendancy to the throne, it should be made clear that Judah had largely turned away from its devotion to Yahweh. Its commitment to worship only Yahweh had fallen into disrepair, and most of its monarchs either practiced idolatry themselves (or worse!) or turned a blind eye and deaf ear to the idolatrous practices and rituals of the people. With the exception of "good King Hezekiah," devotion to Yahweh was, at best, lukewarm, and at worst, nonexistent. This did not bode well for Judah. And it should be emphasized that Josiah's two immediate predecessors, his father Amon and his grandfather Manasseh, were among the most vile of all. A far cry from Hezekiah, Josiah's great-grandfather.

King Josiah changed everything—well, at least in the short-term. In the eighteenth year of his reign, at the age of 26, Josiah authorized that money be spent to repair and refurbish the Temple in Jerusalem. Carpenters, masons and construction workers were employed to complete the renovations. While the work was underway, the high priest Hilkiah discovered a scroll, or parchment—long forgotten—that is often identified as the Book of Deuteronomy. Hilkiah passed the scroll to Shaphan, King Josiah's court scribe, who, in turn, read it to the king:

> When the king heard the book being read, he tore his clothes in dismay, and gave the following order to Hilkiah, the priest, to Ahikam, son of Shaphan, to Achbor, son of Micaiah, to Shaphan, the court secretary, and to Asaiah, the king's attendant: "Go and consult the Lord for me and for all the people of Judah about the teachings of this book. The Lord

> is angry with us because our ancestors have not done what this book says must be done." (2 Kings 22:11-13)

What happened next has proven to be quite enigmatic—and finally leads to the subject of this chapter. While the prophets Jeremiah, Zephaniah and Nahum (three prophets whose preachings, deeds and accomplishments are chronicled in Old Testament books named after them) were ministering during this time period, Josiah's representatives chose *not* to bring the scroll to any of them for analysis and interpretation. Rather...

> Hilkiah, Ahikam, Achbor, Shaphan and Asaiah went to consult a woman named Huldah, a prophet who lived in the newer part of Jerusalem. (Her husband Shallum, the son of Tikvah and grandson of Harhas, was in charge of the Temple robes.) They described to her what had happened, and she told them to go back to the king and give him the following message from the Lord: "I am going to punish Jerusalem and all its people, as written in the book that the king has read. They have rejected Me and have offered sacrifices to other gods, and so have stirred up My anger by all they have done. My anger is aroused against Jerusalem, and it will not die down. As for the king himself, this is what I, the Lord God of Israel, say: You listened to what is written in the book, and you repented and humbled yourself before Me, tearing your clothes and weeping, when you heard how I threatened to punish Jerusalem and its people. I will make it a terrifying sight, a place whose name people will use as a curse. But I have heard your prayer, and the punishment which I am going to bring on Jerusalem will not come until after your death. I will let you die in peace." The men returned to King Josiah with this message. (2 Kings 22:14-20)

Josiah's worst fears were realized, and he set out initiating widespread, wholesale spiritual reforms, which today are known as the "Deuteronomic Reforms," to purge idolatry and restore proper devotion to Yahweh. After all, it was largely the aberrant practices of his father Amon and grandfather Manasseh, among others, that had put Judah in such dire straits.

CONSULTATION WITH HULDAH

As important as the Deuteronomic Reforms were, it is Huldah who merits special consideration. She is mentioned in Scripture in 2 Kings (as quoted above) and in 2 Chronicles 34:22-28, a parallel account to 2 Kings 22. But these accounts convey virtually no information about her, except to list the name of her husband (Shallum), his role in court (keeper of the royal wardrobe) and their home (newer part of Jerusalem). Who is this woman otherwise?

Speculation runs rampant, and the words of Scripture as found in 2 Kings and 2 Chronicles are incredibly short on detail. Clearly Huldah had a pre-existing reputation as either a messenger of God or a woman of deep spirituality—or both. It is thought that she was related to the more prominent prophet Jeremiah—both descendants of Joshua bin Nun of the tribe of Ephraim. Jeremiah, of the tribe of Levi on his father's side, was also of the tribe of Ephraim through his mother. Whether Huldah's notoriety came from her relationship to Jeremiah or emerged from her own sanctity and ministry is also unclear, but her reputation had reached the ears of King Josiah or, if not him, then those of his closest advisors.

Rabbi Nissan Mindel of the Hasidic organization Chasad pointed out that the *Midrash*, an ancient commentary on Hebrew Scripture compiled by Judaic scholars, described Huldah as the administrator and instructor in a yeshiva (school) that taught the word of God to Jewish women. In her 2008 text *Kabbalistic Teachings of the Female Prophets*, J. Zohara Meyerhoff Hieronimus mentioned that Huldah was thought to serve as a librarian, but was, in all likelihood, much more than that—agreeing that she was a teacher of young women. In other quarters, probably due to her husband's profession as royal clothier, Huldah was asserted to be a seamstress.

It is also unknown if King Josiah specifically asked his advisors to bring the scroll directly to Huldah or whether they took it upon themselves to consult her. One school of thought is that Josiah, fearing possibly terrible punishments from the Lord, directed his representatives to visit Huldah in the hope that a woman's interpretation of God's wrath would be more gentle—or that she, as a woman, might beg God to soften His reprisal. No such luck. Huldah's interpretation of the scroll was honest, uncompromising and frightful. The people of Judah would suffer greatly, but God's retribution would be handed down after Josiah's death. It was this forthright pronouncement that served as the catalyst for King Josiah's Deuteronomic Reforms.

As important as Huldah was to the evolution of these Reforms, Professor Claudia V. Camp of Texas Christian University, in *The*

Encyclopedia of Jewish Women (1997), focused on an equally important, albeit different, contribution: "Huldah's...prophetic words of judgment are centered on a written document: she authorizes what will become the core of Scripture for Judaism and Christianity. Her validation of a text thus stands as the first recognizable act in the long process of canon formation. Huldah authenticates a document as being God's word, thereby affording it the sanctity required for establishing a text as authoritative, or canonical."

ANAGRAMS, CODES AND ATHBASH

While detailed information about the personal life of Huldah has been in short supply throughout the ages, an entirely new approach to revealing much more information about Huldah, her ministry and her accomplishments has been devised by author and researcher Preston Kananagh. If the techniques employed by Mr. Kavanagh are as accurate and comprehensive as he believes them to be, then history may very well elevate Huldah to a position of historical and spiritual pre-eminence that has heretofore eluded her.

Mr. Kavanagh's 2012 text *Huldah: The Prophet Who Wrote Hebrew Scripture* uses several linguistic analyses of the Hebrew Scriptures that focus on such literary techniques as anagrams, coded spellings and athbash to identify the authors of Scripture and reveal additional information about their lives and ministries. Anagrams, of course, are a rearrangement of letters—similar to the "Word Jumbles" featured in many daily newspapers. These may conceal one's identity, yet can often be deciphered without too much difficulty. For example, "Liekeze" is an anagram for "Ezekiel" or "Rimmai" for "Miriam."

Coded spellings are, perhaps, slightly more sophisticated as they employ one letter from consecutive words in a text to spell an author's name. As Kavanagh explains, "A five-letter name would draw upon five Hebrew text words in a row. Again, letters could fall in any sequence."

The last technique presented by Kavanagh is a letter-exchange system known as *athbash*, which may befuddle those (such as I!) who do not speak or write Hebrew. As Kavanagh explains, "Athbash generates twenty-one other ways to spell any Hebrew word. It divided the Hebrew alphabet in half to form facing rows of letters. Eleven letters run right-to-left; the other eleven run left-to-right. Next, tractor-tread rotation changes the interfaces, allowing the parallel rows of letters (with one adjustment) to generate twenty-one new ways to spell a name."

Newly devised computer programs have also assisted with the refinement of these techniques, with the likelihood that they will continue to offer additional information and insights in the years ahead. But since the purpose of this chapter is to reflect on the ministry of Huldah, I will confine this chapter to the fascinating portrait that Kavanagh paints of her. Clearly, the fact that he has written an entire book on Huldah when she only appears by name (or so we thought!) in two brief passages in 2 Kings and 2 Chronicles speaks volumes about the quantity of biographical and ministerial information he has compiled by using these research techniques.

Kavanagh's linguistic analysis of the Hebrew Scriptures as they apply to Huldah paint a picture of a woman who was of monumental political and spiritual importance as well as a lightning rod for both praise on the one hand and criticism, disdain and downright contempt on the other. His research suggests that Huldah's presence—either by the words she herself composed or through the codings that refer to her both positively and negatively—span all three sections of the Hebrew Scriptures: the Torah, Neviim and Ketubim. He is also confident that many of the details of her personal life can be historically pinpointed and verified.

QUEEN HULDAH?

According to Kavanagh, it is likely that Huldah was born in 640 BCE and married Shallum ben Tikvah, the king's wardrobe coordinator, during her early to middle teenage years. Marriage during one's teenage years was the norm in Judah during this time period. Therefore, when she was approached by representatives of King Josiah to verify the authenticity of the newly discovered "book of the law" (usually thought to be a portion of Deuteronomy) in 622 BCE, she was already a married woman, but either in her late teens or early twenties. However, a dramatic and sweeping change occurred in her life when she married King Josiah's son Jehoiakim in 616 BCE (at the age of 25) and gave birth to their son Jehoiachin (also known as Jeconiah) in 615 BCE.

Scripture gives no explanation for the termination of Huldah's marriage to Shallum ben Tikvah and her subsequent second marriage to Jehoiakim. Did Shallum die, making Huldah an "available" widow? Was there a divorce, for reasons unknown? Was Huldah in some way "snatched" from her husband as a prerogative of royalty? After all, Kavanagh describes her as "surpassingly attractive—beautiful, skilled, accomplished, and a magnet to men." In the absence of more specific information, this marital transition—for now—must remain a mystery.

Huldah, who is believed to have been related to the great prophet Jeremiah, was the same age as her famous relative. When Jeremiah began to prophesy that God would punish the people of Judea for their apostasy, he fled Jerusalem when banished from the Temple precincts by Huldah's husband, King Jehoiakim. When Jeremiah was joined in his prophetic ministry by the scribe Baruch, it was Baruch who read aloud Jeremiah's predictions to the other scribes of Jerusalem. When Baruch was summoned to read these same predictions a second time to King Jehoiakim, Huldah was present to see her husband burn Baruch's scrolls page by page in utter defiance.

Jehoiakim was considered to be a godless tyrant who aligned himself at different times with both Egypt and Babylon, depending upon which allegiance would be to his greater advantage. Upon his death in 597 BCE at the hands of King Nebuchadnezzar of Babylon—whether as a result of a Babylonian siege of Jerusalem or in a failed escape effort—their son Jehoiachin ascended to the throne of Judea, thus making Huldah the "queen mother." While 2 Kings 24:8 identifies "Nehushta, the daughter of Elnathan from Jerusalem" as the mother of Jehoiachin, Kavanagh disputes this claim, suggesting that Nehushta, which means "snake," may simply have been an insult directed at Huldah or a reference to an Asherah cult Huldah led while in exile in Babylon. (More about that later!)

Jehoiachin's reign in Judea lasted for several short months before Nebuchadnezzar exiled him, his mother Huldah and many members of the royal court of Judah, along with a number of artisans and skilled workers. Jehoiachin's uncle Mattaniah, re-named Zedekiah by Nebuchadnezzar, became the new puppet ruler of Judah and vassal to Babylon.

The next stage of Huldah's life was lived in Babylon and was marked by various accomplishments and controversies. While in Babylon, Huldah, as queen mother, was regarded as one of Judah's elders and, while undoubtedly spending much of her time in the court of Nebuchadnezzar, was also allowed to visit the settlements of the other Judeans in exile. Also banished to Babylon at this same time was the renowned priest and prophet Ezekiel, whose entire prophetic ministry unfolded while in captivity in Babylon. In 592 BCE, Huldah, along with other Judean elders, was present at the dwelling place of Ezekiel while he experienced several of his dramatic and disturbing visions of idolatry in Jerusalem—as well as its dire consequences. It should be noted at this point that Huldah earned a great deal of criticism while in Babylon for leading a cult that honored the Canaanite goddess Asherah as "the queen of heaven." It is quite possible that Huldah was simply following an older Judean tradition, usually orchestrated by the queen mothers, to pay homage to Asherah—and perhaps to view her as the spouse of Yahweh. While some viewed this as a dangerous foray into forbidden idolatry, others viewed it less unfavorably, more as a harmless custom or tradition.

While Huldah and Jehoiachin were exiled in Babylon, King Zedekiah ruled Judah as Nebuchadnezzar's vassal. However, over the course of time, Zedekiah began to take liberties and disregarded his obligations to his Babylonian overlord. He discontinued tribute payments to Nebuchadnezzar and even pursued an alliance with Egypt against Babylon. By 586 BCE, Nebuchadnezzar decided that such disloyalty required a strong response—and initiated a siege of Jerusalem. Parenthetically, the return of Nebuchadnezzar to Judah had been forewarned repeatedly by Jeremiah—and ignored by Zedekiah.

Inexplicably, anagram information placed Huldah in Jerusalem at the time of this siege. Why Huldah would be permitted to leave Babylon while essentially serving as a hostage remains undetermined. It is also unknown whether Jehoiachin accompanied Huldah to Jerusalem or if Huldah unthinkably left Jehoiachin in Babylon while she returned to Jerusalem.

After Nebuchadnezzar's conquest of Judah, the burning of Jerusalem and the exile of most Judeans to Babylon, apparently Huldah (and perhaps Jehoiachin) were permitted to remain in Judah. Nebuchadnezzar appointed Gedaliah, the grandson of Shaphan, who had been a trusted member of King Josiah's court, as governor of Judah, and Gedaliah chose the town of Mizpah, several miles distant from Jerusalem, as his new capital. With his appointment, many Judeans, who had fled their homeland with the arrival of the Babylonian army, returned to Judah with the intention of helping Gedaliah to rebuild their country. However, the assassination of Gedaliah, as well as the slaughter of many of his supporters as well as the Babylonian garrison protecting them in the following year by other Judeans who opposed Gedaliah's alliance with Babylon led the surviving Judean supporters of Gedaliah to fear reprisal by Nebuchadnezzar—and wanted to flee to Egypt. Jeremiah, who was with them, urged them to remain in Judah, promising them that they would not face retribution at the hands of Nebuchadnezzar. But even though they had promised to accede to Jeremiah's counsel, they reneged on their promise, fled to Egypt, and forced Jeremiah to accompany them. Huldah, now 55 years old, was included in this number, and fled to Egypt with the other Judean expatriates. It is possible that Jehoiachin was also present in Egypt.

Despite the fact that they were kinsfolk, Jeremiah and Huldah did not see eye to eye on a number of significant issues. Jeremiah opposed a Judean alliance with Egypt while Huldah promoted it. Jeremiah criticized the worship of Asherah as queen of heaven while Huldah encouraged and, perhaps, even led it. Jeremiah predicted that the idolatry practiced by the Judeans in Egypt would seal their doom in Egypt, but Huldah rejected this.

Kavanagh uncovered evidence that Huldah and the other Judean elders in Egypt contacted a young Persian mercenary leader named Cyrus to aid them in a rebellion against Nebuchadnezzar and a possible re-conquest of Judah. This plot was first hatched in 577 or 576 BCE. Cyrus, years later, would achieve renown as King Cyrus the Great of Persia, but this foray into Judah did not result in any of the long-term successes he enjoyed later in his distinguished career. There seems to be little information available about the specifics of this erstwhile rebellion, but it is possible that the rebel forces may actually have re-captured

Jerusalem and held it for a short time, only to find it re-taken by Nebuchadnezzar's forces or allies in 573 BCE.

Anagrams suggest that Huldah and Cyrus (obviously) survived the battle of Jerusalem, with Huldah first fleeing to Zoar on the periphery of the Dead Sea, and ultimately settling in Bethel, where she lived out her remaining days until she passed in 564 BCE at the age of 76.

Preston Kavanagh's book *Huldah: The Prophet Who Wrote Hebrew Scripture* (2012) uses today's technology to offer a heretofore unexplored interpretation of the composition of the Hebrew Scriptures, especially as they apply to Huldah, a prophetess barely mentioned in 2 Kings and 2 Chronicles. If Kavanagh's analysis of the anagrams, codings and athbash is to be accepted as "Gospel" (no pun intended!), then Huldah must be elevated from relative obscurity to a prominence commensurate with her literary accomplishments. The 1,773 anagrams about Huldah (and so much additional coding) suggest that Huldah appeared either as a figure or as an author in a staggering number of Old Testament books, including (but not necessarily confined to) Genesis, Exodus, Leviticus, Numbers, Joshua, Judges, Ruth, 1 and 2 Samuel, 2 Kings, 1 Chronicles, Ezra, Job, Psalms, Proverbs, Song of Songs, Isaiah, Jeremiah, Lamentations, Ezekiel, Daniel, Joel, Habakkuk and Wisdom.

In addition, Kavanagh's analysis of the Hebrew Scriptures has led him to identify Huldah as the author of the following popular Biblical citations, perhaps among many, many others:

How the mighty have fallen. (2 Samuel 1:19)

I have escaped by the skin of my teeth. (Job 19:20)

Your people will be my people and your God shall be my God. (Ruth 1:16)

And let Us make man in Our image, after Our likeness. (Genesis 1:26)

Only time—and additional scholarship and revelations—will tell whether Huldah remains in relative Biblical obscurity or rises to greater prominence as both a literary and prophetic giant.

QUESTIONS FOR REVIEW

1. What were the consequences of Rehoboam's refusal to yield to the Israelites' request of relaxation of taxes and conscription?

2. What impact did the Assyrian conquest of Israel have on the worship practices of the Israelites (or Samaritans)?

3. What separated the reign of King Hezekiah from the reigns of the other Judean kings who preceded and followed him?

4. In what way did Huldah contribute to the establishment of the "Deuteronomic Reforms" of King Josiah?

5. Why was Huldah selected to evaluate the contents of the discovered scroll?

6. What is *athbash* and how is it used to shed light on the life and ministry of Huldah?

7. According to Preston Kavanagh, what became of Huldah's marriage to Shallum ben Tikvah?

8. What chain of events led to Huldah's re-settlement in Babylon? What was controversial about her activities in Babylon?

9. In what ways did Huldah disagree with her cousin, the prophet Jeremiah?

10. According to Kavanagh, what are Huldah's *real* accomplishments as a prophetess?

Chapter Ten
NOADIAH

Chapters 11 and 12 introduced two women prophets about whom no more than a single sentence in Scripture is written—and yet, from that single mention (with a little help from 21st century technology), a great deal of important information has been extrapolated. The story of the prophetess Noadiah is much more of the same. In this case, Noadiah appears when the Judeans had been permitted to return to their homeland by the Persians, who had conquered the Babylonians, who had previously deported and enslaved them. This is the time period of the architect and future governor Nehemiah, whose words of petition to God are not words of support and solace:

> *I prayed, "God, remember what Tobiah and Sanballat have done and punish them. Remember that woman Noadiah and all the other prophets who tried to frighten me." (Nehemiah 6:14)*

Clearly, Nehemiah and Noadiah are on opposite sides of the fence. Well, in this case, it's really more than a fence—it's a wall. What is the source of the chasm between these two, and why do many Biblical scholars label Noadiah a "false" prophetess? It would appear that some background information is necessary to understand the nature of this dispute.

NEHEMIAH'S RETURN TO JUDAH

As mentioned above, the southern kingdom of Judah was conquered by the Babylonian forces under King Nebuchadnezzar in 586 BCE, and most of the inhabitants of Judah were hauled off to Babylon to serve as slaves. A few disparate Judeans remained behind, but the land had become desolate, and Jerusalem was no more than a smoldering pile of ruins. When the Babylonians were, in turn, conquered by the Persians in 539 BCE, the Judeans both home and abroad in Judah and in Babylon, respectively, now found themselves under the rule of Persia. Happily for them, the Persians did not look upon their Judean subjects as either enemies or slaves, and welcomed them as full citizens of the Persian Empire, even permitting the Judeans who had been enslaved in Babylon to return to their homeland—an offer many Judeans gratefully accepted. Those who returned to Judah became known as "the remnant"—a name, you may recall, that was foreshadowed by Isaiah in the naming of his firstborn son Shearjashub, which meant "a remnant shall return."

As the Judeans began to rebuild their homeland and re-establish their faith, Nehemiah was serving the Persian king Artaxerxes II in the Persian capital city of Susa, in modern-day Iran. While his position as royal cupbearer may seem rather mundane, it was an important role that demonstrated its holder was greatly trusted and respected by the reigning monarch and royal family.

When Nehemiah received reports from Judah that the walls and gates of Jerusalem were still in utter disrepair and the Judeans were the objects of disdain on the part of their non-Judean neighbors, it caused him great distress. Eventually his discomfort was noticed by King Artaxerxes II, who gave him permission to journey to Judah to facilitate reconstruction. The king even ordered a cavalry troop to accompany and protect him. However, when Nehemiah's plans to rebuild the walls of Jerusalem were revealed, he encountered opposition and derision:

> *But Sanballat, from the town of Beth Horon, and Tobiah, an official in the province of Ammon, heard that someone had come to work for the good of the people of Israel, and they were highly indignant...When Sanballat, Tobiah, and an Arab named Geshem heard what we were planning to do, they laughed at us and said, "What do you think you're doing?..." (Nehemiah 2:10,19)*

Apparently Sanballat, Tobiah and Geshem served as provincial governors within the Persian Empire—most likely from Samaria (to the north), Ammon (to the east) and Kedem (to the southeast). They conspired to disrupt the reconstruction of the wall around Jerusalem through a variety of stratagems directed against Nehemiah—they threatened him with physical harm, spread rumors about him to damage his reputation, misled him via false prophets and tried to turn other Judeans against him. But all of their efforts failed, and the wall was rebuilt in record time—within 52 days.

How does the prophetess Noadiah play into this melodrama, and why would she oppose such an improvement in Jerusalem's reconstruction? Actually, the probable answer—and lacking a more specific rationale in Scripture means that the reason behind her opposition is conjectural—has less to do with Jerusalem's defense and more to do with its social structure and family life.

The Book of Ezra immediately precedes the Book of Nehemiah in the corpus of the *Hebrew Scriptures*, suggesting that Ezra, as a representative of the Persian Empire whose responsibility it was to administer and direct the religious practices of Judaism, arrived in Judah prior to Nehemiah. Biblical historians are not in agreement on this issue, some thinking that Nehemiah's arrival may have come first. In any event, it was Ezra who enforced a much stricter interpretation of Judaic practices in Judah that were considered quite disruptive by some of the local inhabitants. His goal was to purge Judah of "foreign influences" that may have corrupted the proper practices of Judaism:

> *Ezra the priest stood up and spoke...He said, "You have been faithless and have brought guilt on Israel by marrying foreign women. Now then, confess your sins to the Lord, the God of your ancestors, and do what pleases Him.*
>
> *Separate yourselves from the foreigners living in our land and get rid of your foreign wives...[A list of all the men of Judah with foreign*

wives was then compiled]...*All these men had foreign wives. They divorced them and sent them and their children away."* (Ezra 10:10-11, 44)

Dr. Wilda C. Gafney noted in her book *Daughters of Miriam: Women Prophets of Ancient Israel* (2008) that Nehemiah's wall around Jerusalem was not used for defensive purposes insofar as Jerusalem and its surrounding land of Judah —as well as the surrounding non-Judaic territories—were all coexisting provinces within the much larger Persian Empire. Border walls were as unnecessary as walls constructed to separate one state from another within the United States today. These Persian provinces were not in enmity with one another.

The last chapter of the Book of Nehemiah demonstrates that Ezra and Nehemiah saw eye-to-eye on this issue of foreign corruption:

At that time I also discovered that many of the Jewish men had married women from Ashdod, Ammon and Moab. Half of their children spoke the language of Ashdod or some other language and didn't know how to speak our language. I reprimanded the men, called down curses on them, beat them, and pulled out their hair. Then I made them take an oath in God's name that never again would they or their children intermarry with foreigners. I told them, "It was foreign women that made King Solomon sin. Here was a man who was greater than any of the kings of other nations. God loved him and made him king over all of Israel, and yet he fell into this sin. Are we then to follow your example and disobey our God by marrying foreign women?" (Nehemiah 13:23-27)

ONE WALL, TWO VIEWPOINTS

It is quite possible that Noadiah saw this rampart surrounding Jerusalem as a concrete (no pun intended!) way to enforce this separation of the practitioners of Judaism from their family members who did not share their faith. Noadiah clearly held a special place among those who were opposed to the wall. As Dr. Gafney also pointed out, "Noadiah was a prominent leader of the prophetic opposition to Nehemiah...she had all of the other prophets in Jerusalem on her side...her opposition was formidable enough to send Nehemiah to appeal to YHWH, and...Nehemiah was terrified of what she could or would do if YHWH did not intervene."

Again we are tasked with analyzing the contributions of a prophetess of the Old Testament about whom so little—one tiny reference!—has been written in Scripture. Was Noadiah a "false" prophetess? I would respectfully disagree with that assessment. If anything, I think it can be concluded that she and Nehemiah both looked at the same reality from different perspectives. Is this another possible example of an important woman in Judaic history being overlooked? I think that is very likely the case. If Noadiah's stature was so great that she was singled out by name by Nehemiah, then she was a woman who clearly should have been featured more prominently in Scripture. Unfortunately, this is a snub we've seen too many times already.

QUESTIONS FOR REVIEW

1. What circumstances led Nehemiah to return to Jerusalem from the court of Artaxerxes II?

2. What role did Noadiah play in the daily life of Judah?

3. What were Noadiah's objections to Nehemiah's plans? Were her objections well-founded?

4. Why are her objections viewed as social rather than defensive?

Chapter Eleven
ESTHER

If Abigail was an abused wife of Nabal in chapter 7—and it would not be a far-fetched assumption to make about her in light of her husband's unreasonable demeanor, violent temper and frequent alcoholic stupor—then it may be argued that the marriage of Esther to King Ahaseurus was even worse (or, at least, comparably unsavory). For it's possible that Esther can be viewed with jealousy as the queen of Persia or with pity as an abductee who was sexually violated. It is quite possible that neither the marriage of Abigail nor of Esther was quite "made in heaven."

Like many of the preceding stories of the Old Testament prophetesses and their ministries, a degree of background information is necessary to fully understand the cesspool of intrigue into which Esther was placed. Right off the top, there are two different versions of the story of Esther—one written in Hebrew and the other written in Greek. The Greek version, written later than the Hebrew, offers additional information not found in the Hebrew account and differs in some of its details. So the accuracy of the story of Esther is immediately called into question. Additionally, Biblical scholars, in analyzing Esther, have been unable to identify its author or even determine if the author's intention was to record historical fact or present an historically-rooted novella. The Book of Esther shows the author's understanding of Persian laws and customs but clashes at times with other historical data known to be objectively accurate. So, how is the story of Esther to be interpreted? That question is as debatable as the accuracy of its content!

THE VASHTI CONTROVERSY

The story of Esther actually begins at a royal banquet thrown by King Ahasuerus of Persia in his capital city of Susa, in modern-day Iran. The first problem with this story is the actual identity of the king. The king known as Ahasuerus in the Hebrew Scriptures is usually considered to be King Xerxes I, the son of King Darius and grandson of King Cyrus the Great. If so, that would place the beginning of this story at approximately 483 BCE, in the third year of his reign. However, other Biblical scholars believe that Ahasuerus may actually be an alternative name for any one of three kings who followed Xerxes on the Persian throne of the Archaemenid Dynasty at different times over the next 145 years or so—Artaxerxes I (465-425 BCE), Artaxerxes II (404-359 BCE) or Artaxerxes III (359-338 BCE). It is believed that both the names "Ahasuerus" and "Xerxes" are derived from the Persian word *Xsayarsa,* translated as "ruler of kings." Still other Biblical scholars view the story of Esther largely as a fabrication to explain the etiology of the Jewish festival of Purim. So we are left, perhaps, with more questions than answers, but the story of Esther—fact or fiction—is still a compelling and dramatic story in its own right.

When the story begins, King Xerxes, ruler of a vast empire stretching from India to Ethiopia, hosted a lavish banquet designed to showcase his vast wealth.

> *In the third year of his reign, he [Xerxes] gave a banquet for all of his officials and administrators. The armies of Persia and Media were present, as well as the governors and noblemen of the [127] provinces. For six whole months he made a show of the riches of the imperial court with all its splendor and majesty.*
>
> *After that, the king gave a banquet for all the men in the capital city of Susa, rich and poor alike. It lasted a whole week and was held in the gardens of the royal palace...Drinks were served in gold cups, no two of them alike, and the king was generous with the royal wine. There were no limitations on the drinks; the king had given orders to the palace servants that everyone could have as much as he wanted. Meanwhile, inside the royal palace Queen Vashti was giving a banquet for the women. (Esther 1:5-9)*

At this point in the narrative, Xerxes is portrayed as a gracious and beneficent monarch who treats his staff and fellow citizens with generosity and magnanimity, but the circumstances—possibly driven by alcoholic over-consumption—quickly turn.

> *On the seventh day of his banquet the king was drinking and feeling happy, so he called in the seven eunuchs who were his personal servants,*

> Mehuman, Biztha, Harbona, Bigtha, Abagtha, Zethar and Carkas. He ordered them to bring in Queen Vashti, wearing her royal crown. The queen was a beautiful woman, and the king wanted to show off her beauty to the officials and all of his guests. But when the servants told Queen Vashti of the king's command, she refused to come. This made the king furious. (Esther 1:10-12)

No reason is given for the queen's refusal to comply. Perhaps she thought it rude to abandon her own guests. Perhaps she resented being ordered about. Perhaps her royal dignity was offended by being showcased as a trophy. Regardless of her motivation, her failure to comply caused Xerxes a great deal of embarrassment—embarrassment that needed to be addressed.

> Now it was the king's custom to ask for expert opinion on questions of law and order, so he called for his advisers, who would know what should be done...seven officials of Persia and Media who held the highest offices in the kingdom. He said to these men, "I, King Xerxes, sent my servants to Queen Vashti with a command, and she refused to obey it! What does the law say we should do with her?" Then Memucan [one of the advisers] declared..."Queen Vashti has insulted not only the king but...every man in the empire! Every woman in the empire will start looking down on her husband as soon as she hears what the queen has done...Wives everywhere will have no respect for their husbands, and husbands will be angry with their wives.
>
> If it please Your Majesty, issue a royal proclamation that Vashti may never again appear before the king. Have it written into the laws of Persia and Media so that it can never be changed. Then give her place as queen to some better woman. When your proclamation is made

> known...every woman will treat her husband with proper respect, whether he's rich or poor." (Esther 1:13-20)

Xerxes followed Memucan's suggestion.

> To each of the royal provinces he sent a message in the language and the system of writing of that province, saying that every husband should be the master of his home and speak with final authority. (Esther 1:22)

It goes without saying that such a decree in today's society would be viewed with outrage, protests and total non-compliance—not to mention outright rejection by our own Supreme Court. We would view it as nothing less than chauvinistic paranoia run amok. But times and attitudes at that time in that part of the world were very different. Perhaps the outmoded notion that "the husband is king of his castle" can be traced all the way back to this moment in fictionalized Persian history!

After Queen Vashti had been dismissed from the royal household, Xerxes continued to receive related suggestions from his closest advisers.

> Why don't you make a search to find some beautiful young virgins? You can appoint officials in every province of the empire and have them bring all these beautiful young girls to your harem here in Susa...Put them in the care of Hegai, the eunuch who is in charge of your women, and let them be given a beauty treatment. Then take the girl you like best and make her queen in Vashti's place. (Esther 2:2-4)

THE ROUNDUP OF VIRGINS

Xerxes followed this advice, and it was because of this decision that Esther entered the picture. Esther, whose Hebrew name was Hadassah, was a beautiful young woman who lived in Susa with her much older cousin, Mordecai. The Book of Esther describes Mordecai as a man from Jerusalem who was taken to Babylon with King Jehoiachin and his family in 597 BCE at the time Jehoiachin surrendered his crown to Nebuchadnezzar to save the people of Jerusalem and Judah from invasion. However, this statement is clearly in error, in that Mordecai would have to have been over 100 years old for the chronology to fit. Regardless, upon the death of Esther's parents, Mordecai adopted her and raised her as his own daughter.

It was as a result of this "roundup" of young virgins that Esther found herself in the royal palace under the supervision of the eunuch Hegai. Fortunately, Esther found favor with Hegai, who gave her special treatment as one of his favorite charges.

Mordecai was also in the employ of King Xerxes at this time in a low administrative post, and was able to remain in contact with Esther each day. On his advice, Esther did not reveal to anyone that she was of Judean heritage and worshipped Yahweh.

The beauty treatments administered to the young women in Hegai's care lasted for a year, and then each girl would be taken in turn to spend the night with King Xerxes. After her night with the king, the girl would then be taken to another harem composed of the king's concubines. Concubines were women who were held in lower status than wives, but whose function was to provide men of power (such as the king) with both pleasure and additional heirs.

Once placed in the harem for concubines, a young woman would not return to the king unless he summoned her by name. And it came to pass that Esther's turn had arrived.

> *The time came for Esther to go to the king. Esther—the daughter of Abihail and the cousin of Mordecai, who had adopted her as his daughter; Esther—admired by everyone who saw her. When her turn came, she wore just what Hegai…advised her to wear. So in Xerxes' seventh year as king, in the tenth month…Esther was brought to King Xerxes in the royal palace. The king liked her more than any of the other girls, and more than any of the others she won his favor and affection. He placed the royal crown on her head and made her queen in place of Vashti. Then the king gave a great banquet in Esther's honor and invited all his officials and administrators. (Esther 2:15-18)*

It should be noted as this point that Esther had been given no choice about joining Hegai's harem, nor did she have a choice regarding an "overnight visit" with the king. To that extent, Esther may rightfully be described as an abductee who was sexually violated. Author and artist Rachel Friedlander put it quite bluntly in her monograph "Five Things About Esther That Nobody Talks About" (2019) when she pointed out, "She was taken captive…She was raped." It is quite possible, however, that Xerxes developed genuine feelings of affection for Esther in that he made her his queen, but whether those feelings blossomed into authentic love or a shallower type of infatuation is unclear. While the Hebrew version of the Book of Esther says *"the king* liked *her more than any of the other girls"* (2:17), the Greek version reports that *"he* fell in love *with Esther, who pleased him more than any of the others..."* (2:17). Clearly, Xerxes' depth of emotion toward Esther will remain a mystery.

HAMAN, MORDECAI AND THE THREAT OF GENOCIDE

The story then took several important and dramatic turns. The first of these centered around an assassination plot gone awry.

> *During the time that Mordecai held office in the palace, Bigthana and Teresh, two of the palace eunuchs who guarded the entrance to the king's rooms, became hostile to King Xerxes and plotted to assassinate him. Mordecai learned about it and told Queen Esther, who then told the king what Mordecai had found out. There was an investigation, and it was discovered that the report was true, so both men were hanged on the gallows. The king ordered an account of this to be written down in the official records of the empire. (Esther 2:21-23)*

The significance of the recording of this episode in the imperial annals will come to light a little later in the narrative. But, in the meantime, King Xerxes appointed a man named Haman to serve as his new viceroy, or prime minister. Haman, the son of Hammedatha, was a descendant of the Amalekite king, Agag. Historically, the Amalekites and Israelites were bitter enemies, and one of King Saul of Israel's first military campaigns was against the Amalekites, whose culture he largely annihilated. So it is quite possible that Haman arrived on the scene in Persia with hostile feelings toward any Judeans residing in the empire. If so, these feelings only grew deeper:

> *The king ordered all the officials in his service to show their respect for Haman by kneeling and bowing to him. They all did so, except for Mordecai, who refused...The other officials asked him why he was disobeying the king's command...but he would not listen to them." I am a Jew," he explained, "and I cannot bow to Haman." So they told Haman about this...Haman was furious...and when he learned that Mordecai was a Jew, he decided to do more than punish Mordecai alone. He made plans to kill every Jew in the whole Persian Empire. (Esther 3:2-6)*

Clearly Haman was an arrogant, vindictive man who had no qualms about executing thousands of innocent people to satisfy his own ego, but to implement his plan he would have to secure the king's permission. That would involve a two-part plan. The first part involved lying to the king, and the second was bribing him.

> *So Haman told the king, "There is a certain race of people scattered all over your empire and found in every province. They observe customs that are not like those of any other people. Moreover, they do not obey the laws of the empire, so it is not in your best interests to tolerate them. If it please Your Majesty, issue a decree that they are to be put to death. If you do, I guarantee that I will be able to put 375 tons of silver into the royal treasury for the administration of the empire." (Esther 3:8-9)*

To select the day for this massive execution of the Judeans, Haman cast lots, called *purim*, to determine the day and month.

The date chosen at random in this way was the thirteenth day of the month of Adar. The king gave his approval and told Haman:

> *The people and their money are yours; do as you like with them. So...Haman called the king's secretaries and dictated a proclamation to be translated into every language and system of writing used in the empire and to be sent to all the rulers, governors and officials. It was issued in the name of King Xerxes and stamped with his ring...It contained the instructions that...on the thirteenth day of Adar, all Jews —young and old, women and children—were to be killed. They were to be slaughtered without mercy and their belongings were to be taken. The contents of the proclamation were to be made public in every province, so that everyone would be prepared when the day came.* (Esther 3:11-14)

It should be noted that Persian law was very exacting. Once a law was passed or a proclamation was announced, it could *not* be rescinded. So the fate of the Judeans was sealed—and now that these events were set in motion, they were irreversible.

Bad news travels fast, and the Judean population within Persia was in a state of panic - and clearly not without good reason.

> *Throughout all the provinces, wherever the king's proclamation was made known, there was loud mourning among the Jews. They fasted, wept, wailed and most of them put on sackcloth and lay in ashes.* (Esther 4:3)

Mordecai, when he heard the news as it was proclaimed in Susa, behaved in exactly the same way. He passed word of the proclamation and its consequences to Hathach, one of Queen Esther's servants, to relay to her, along with the request that she beg the king to show mercy on the people of Judah. Esther's response was less than what he hoped to hear:

> *If anyone, man or woman, goes to the inner courtyard and sees the king without being summoned, that person must die. That is the law; everyone, from the king's advisers to the people in the provinces, knows that. There is only one way to get around this law: if the king holds out his gold scepter to someone, then that person's life is spared. But it has been a month since the king sent for me. (Esther 4:11)*

Mordecai wasn't exactly pleased with Esther's response, and he lodged a second appeal, accompanied by a warning:

> *Don't imagine that you are safer than any other Jew just because you are in the royal palace. If you keep quiet at a time like this, help will come from heaven to the Jews, and they will be saved, but you will die and your father's family will come to an end. Yet who knows—maybe it was for a time like this that you were made queen! (Esther 4:13-14)*

ESTHER'S REQUEST FOR PRAYERS AND FASTING...AND COURAGE

Esther's response to Mordecai was to request that he gather the Judeans who lived in Susa together for three days of fast and prayer in support of her, and she and her servants would do likewise.

> *After that I will go to the king, even though it is against the law. If I must die for doing it, I will die. (Esther 4:16)*

It was this request for supportive fasting and prayers from the Judean population that led to Esther's designation as a prophetess in the *Babylonian Talmud*. To paraphrase Dr. Gaffney, who addressed this issue earlier, prophecy is, among other things "...the proclamation and/or performance of a divine word by a religious intermediary to an individual or community" such as "engaging in intercessory prayer...resolving disputes, etc." In the eyes of the rabbinic scholars, Esther clearly met their definition of "prophet."

Mordecai honored Esther's request and Esther fulfilled her promise. She entered the king's inner courtyard, facing the very real possibility of immediate execution, but was met with a royal reprieve:

> When the king saw Queen Esther standing outside, she won his favor, and he held out to her the gold scepter...."What is it, Queen Esther?" the king asked. "Tell me what you want and you shall have it—even if it is half my empire." Esther replied, "If it please Your Majesty, I would like you and Haman to be my guests tonight at a banquet I am preparing for you." (Esther 5:2-4)

King Xerxes and Haman attended Esther's banquet, and the king again asked Esther what she wanted from him—even if it were half his empire. But Esther responded that she would like the king and Haman to attend a second banquet on the following night, at which time she would make her request. Had Esther developed "cold feet" in failing to petition the king, or was Divine Providence staying her hand? Because, as it turned out, the twenty-four hour delay caused by the second banquet proved to be very fortuitous.

Haman was quite pleased to have been singled out for personal inclusion in both royal banquets, but his mood quickly changed when he left the first banquet and encountered Mordecai near the palace gates. When Mordecai again failed to proffer any sign of respect for Haman, Haman was furious. When he returned home, he vented his anger to his wife, who suggested he immediately have a gallows constructed for Mordecai, and petition the king to have him executed. Haman authorized its immediate construction, and left to make his appeal to the king.

It was on this same evening that the king suffered from a bout of insomnia, so he requested that his court scribe read to him portions of the official imperial records, in the hope that it would help him to fall asleep. As luck (or fate) would have it, the scribe read the account of the assassination plot against him that was uncovered by Mordecai.

> The king asked, "How have we honored and rewarded Mordecai for this?" His servants answered, "Nothing has been done for him." (Esther 6:3)

And it was at this moment that Haman entered the king's courtyard, seeking an audience with the king to secure Mordecai's death—and the conversation that followed deteriorated into a classic example of both arrogance and misunderstanding when the king asked Haman:

> "There is someone I wish very much to honor. What should I do for this man?"
>
> Haman thought to himself, "Now who could the king want to honor so much?
>
> Me, of course." So he answered the king, "Have royal robes brought for this man—robes that you yourself wear. Have a royal ornament put on your own horse. Then have one of your highest noblemen dress the man in these robes and lead him, mounted on the horse, through the city square. Have the nobleman announce as they go: 'See how the king rewards a man he wishes to honor.'" (Esther 6:6-9)

Haman was quite pleased with himself and his brilliant ploy to garner even more accolades and adulation from the people of Susa. But that self-satisfaction ended rather abruptly with the next words of the king:

> Hurry and get the robes and the horse, and provide these honors for Mordecai the Jew. Do everything for him that you have suggested. You will find him sitting at the entrance of the palace. (Esther 6:10)

THE TABLES ARE TURNED

This was Haman's worst nightmare—not only to see the man he wanted dead now honored by the same king he hoped would condemn him to death, but to have to serve as the herald for his nemesis—and listen to him receive the applause and praise that Haman truly believed he deserved instead. As far as he was concerned, his humiliation couldn't be greater. But he was wrong. The worst was yet to come.

Palace eunuchs arrived to escort Haman to his second banquet with King Xerxes and Queen Esther, and Haman was pleased to attend. Xerxes again asked Esther if she had a request to make of him, and Esther replied:

> "If it please Your Majesty to grant my humble request, my wish is that I may live and that my people may live. My people and I have been sold for slaughter...we are about to be destroyed—exterminated!"
>
> Then King Xerxes asked Queen Esther, "Who dares to do such a thing? Where is this man?" Esther answered, "Our enemy, our persecutor, is this evil man Haman!" (Esther 7:3-6)

As Esther explained the circumstances leading up to Xerxes' proclamation, the king realized that he had been deceived by Haman to authorize the destruction of an innocent Judean population—including both his queen and the man who saved his life—and his fury knew no bounds. When he was informed by his servants that Haman had constructed a gallows to hang Mordecai, the solution was quite simple:

> "Hang Haman on it!" the king commanded. (Esther 7:9)

However, the death of Haman did not, in and of itself, solve the problem faced by the Judeans—the upcoming genocide directed against them. As Xerxes himself explained to Esther:

> A proclamation issued in the king's name and stamped with the royal seal cannot be revoked. (Esther 8:8)

Xerxes gave Esther and Mordecai permission to draft another proclamation of their own choosing to help the Judean population—and issue it in the king's name with the king's own royal seal. So they drafted a proclamation allowing the Judeans in every corner of the Persian Empire to defend themselves against any and all attacks—and to take possession of the personal property of anyone who attacked them. In different quarters of the Persian Empire—including the capital city of Susa—those who attacked the Judeans were vanquished, but the Judeans did not plunder their property, even though they were permitted to do so.

Mordecai grew in stature and became an important administrator under King Xerxes—second only to the king in power. It was through his efforts—along with the support of Queen Esther—that an annual festival was created to celebrate the victory over genocide that the Judeans had circumvented. This celebration would be held annually on the fourteenth and fifteenth days of the month of Adar, and became known as *Purim*, calling attention to the casting of lots that would have—but didn't—lead to the annihilation of the Judean population by Haman.

The story of Esther is an inspirational one—whether it is fact or fiction. Esther was a young girl who was thrust into a volatile situation beyond her control and put her life on the line when the situation demanded it. Whether or not she meets the textbook understanding of "prophet" may be a debatable point (perhaps not in the eyes of the Talmudic rabbis!), but there is no reason why she cannot be revered as a role model and heroine.

QUESTIONS FOR REVIEW

I. What is the level of historical accuracy in the story of Queen Esther of Persia?

2. Why did Queen Vashti lose her favored position in the royal court?

3. Is it accurate to label Esther a victim in this story?

4. What reason did Haman have for his dislike of the people of Judah?

5. Was Mordecai justified in the way he related to Haman?

6. On what basis does the Talmud consider Esther to be a prophetess?

7. What decision of King Xerxes caused Haman unexpected embarrassment?

8. How was the genocide of the people of Judah averted?

PROPHETS "ON THE BUBBLE"

Chapter Twelve
REBEKAH

*D*ifferent individuals, as they read the Bible, are left, perhaps, with very different viewpoints regarding its stories, its messages and its protagonists. The details of one episode or the actions of one character may resonate with one reader, yet make little difference to another. Such is the way that literature can impact on our lives—or not.

A woman of importance worthy of discussion for possible inclusion in the roster of Old Testament prophetesses is a contemporary of the matriarch Sarah—her daughter-in-law Rebekah, the wife of her son Isaac. As with Sarah, even casual readers of Scripture are probably familiar with Rebekah—and remember most especially the story of her efforts to trick her husband Isaac into giving his special primogenitary blessing (a blessing reserved for the eldest son) not to his first-born son Esau, but to his second-born son Jacob. And also like Sarah, Rebekah is usually not considered to be a prophetess, except by the

Talmudic scholars of over a millennium ago, who believe she fulfills the criteria for "prophetic inclusion." The Rev. Lindsay Hardin Freeman, an Episcopalian priest who has written extensively about the women of the Bible, admitted in a 2012 blog, "I've overlooked Rebekah...like an apple on the kitchen counter that sits there day after day...Yet she is one of the most important women in the Bible...Without her actions, through which she suffered great loss, the story of God's people might have ended very differently. Much like Mary, Jesus' mother, the future of a people was in her hands." On the strength of Rev. Freeman's comments, certainly a closer look at Rebekah is warranted.

A MARRIAGE MADE IN HEAVEN?

The story of Rebekah begins shortly after the death of Sarah and her burial in Machpelah Cave in the land of Canaan. Abraham called his oldest and most trusted servant to perform a task for him:

> *I want you to make a vow in the name of the Lord, the God of heaven and earth, that you will not choose a wife for my son from the people here in Canaan. You must go back to the country where I was born and get a wife for my son Isaac from among my relatives. (Genesis 24:3-4)*

Abraham further instructed his unnamed servant not to take Isaac with him, but assured him that God would send an angel ahead of him to enable him to find a wife. Abraham's servant made his vow, and set off for the land of Mesopotamia (present-day Iraq) with ten camels. Abraham, you may recall, came originally from Mesopotamia, which was also called Chaldea, before following God's instructions to relocate to the land of Canaan. Abraham's brother and sister-in-law, Nahor and Milcah, lived in Mesopotamia along with their children and grandchildren.

Abraham's servant arrived near the home of Abraham's brother late in the afternoon. He stopped at a well on the outskirts of the city and made the camels kneel in the sand. Looking for guidance from above, he prayed:

> *Lord, God of my master Abraham, give me success today and keep Your promise to my master. Here I am at the well where the young women of the city will be coming to get water. I will say to one of them, "Please, lower your jar and let me have a drink." If she says, "Drink, and I will also bring water for your camels," may she be the one that You have chosen for Your servant Isaac. If this happens, I will know that You have kept Your promise to my master. (Genesis 24:12-14)*

While Abraham's servant was still praying, Rebekah arrived at the well. She was the granddaughter of Nahor and Milcah, the daughter of their son Bethuel, and was described as being *a very beautiful young girl and still a virgin. (Genesis 24:16)* Rebekah was most probably in her teenage years. When Rebekah volunteered not only to provide him with a drink but also to bring water for all of the camels, Abraham's servant was delighted. He:

> *...took an expensive gold ring and put it in her nose and put two large gold bracelets on her arms. (Genesis 24:22)*

Rebekah's unsolicited offer to provide water for the ten camels accompanying Abraham's servant was a *huge* sacrifice. It was not uncommon for camels, nicknamed "ships of the desert" to drink 20 to 30 gallons of water at a time. So this sign that the servant had chosen to indicate God's choice of a wife for Isaac was an incredibly demanding and time-consuming one. Rachel's willingness to perform such a task without outside prompting or compulsion was a real indication of her generosity of spirit. This moment also signifies the first time in the Bible that God is petitioned to choose someone's spouse.

When Rebekah introduced herself as the daughter of Bethuel and the granddaughter of Nahor and Milcah, and told the servant that there was plenty of room and food for the servant, the camels and other servants in his party to spend the night at her home, the servant knelt down and offered another prayer—this one of praise and gratitude to the Lord for leading him directly to Abraham's family. Upon arrival at the house of Bethuel, the servant also met Rebekah's brother Laban, who helped them tend to the camels. But the servant wanted to get straight to the point of his visit:

> *I am the servant of Abraham...The Lord has greatly blessed my master and made him a rich man...Sarah, my master's wife, bore him a son when she was old, and my master has given everything he owns to him. My master made me promise with a vow to obey his command... [to]...go to my father's people, to my relatives, and choose a wife for him. (Genesis 24:34-38)*

The servant explained his prayer to God and the sign he hoped to receive from God (the offer to water the camels) that He would help him to find the right spouse for Isaac. Believing that this marriage was ordained by God, Rebekah's mother and brother agreed to the marriage (Rachel's father Bethuel had already died), but also summoned Rebekah to express her thoughts and feelings. When Rebekah agreed to leave with the servant to marry Isaac, her family sent her off with a blessing:

> *May you, sister, become the mother of millions! May your descendants conquer the cities of their enemies! (Genesis 24:60)*

And Rebekah set off, accompanied by several servant girls of her own along with Abraham's servants, to begin her new wedded life in Canaan. But it should be noted that two singular events accompanied this departure. First, Rebekah's wishes were taken into consideration when the subject of marriage to Isaac came up. It was a rarity at that time in that culture for a young unmarried girl to be given *any* input, rather than having this decision made for her by her family, And second, Rebekah is given a blessing from her family at the moment she departs for Canaan. This is the first time the Bible records one individual (in this case two—Laban and Rebekah's mother) blessing another.

As Rebekah's journey came to its end, Isaac saw the approach of the party and went to greet them. Isaac brought Rebekah into the tent that Sarah had used before her death—and the two were married. Even better than that—they fell in love.

Over the course of time, Abraham remarried, and his second wife Keturah gave him other children. While Abraham provided his other children with gifts, he bequeathed everything he owned to Isaac. When Abraham died at the age of 175, he was buried in the Machpelah Cave in Canaan, alongside his wife Sarah. Ishmael, Abraham's son by Sarah's slave girl Hagar, also prospered and fathered twelve sons.

> The descendants of Ishmael lived in the territory between Havilah and Shur, to the east of Egypt on the way to Assyria. They lived apart from the other descendants of Abraham. (Genesis 25:18)

The Roman-Jewish historian Flavius Josephus (whose birth name was Yosef ben Matityahu), in his text *Antiquities of the Jews*, recorded that Ismael's descendants "...inhabit the lands which are between [the river] Euphrates and the Red Sea, the name of which country is Nabathaea." Other ancient accounts also viewed Ishmael's descendants as the founders of Mecca, Arabia, the progenitors of the Arab population, and the direct ancestors of the prophet Muhammad.

A PREGNANCY—AND A GLIMPSE INTO THE FUTURE

In Canaan, the marriage of Isaac and Rebekah was a loving one but, unfortunately, not one blessed with children. Genesis records that Isaac was forty years old when he married Rebekah, who was probably a teenager at the time, but years passed and Rebekah grew despondent that she was still childless. As Sue and Larry Richards pointed out in their 1999 text *Every Woman in the Bible*, "As the years passed and Rebekah remained childless, she became more and more concerned. Most women in the ancient world saw childbearing as the most fulfilling role in their lives, and Rebekah was no different...She desperately wanted children and had none."

In circumstances such as this, a man might choose to take on a second wife or, in the case of Isaac's father Abraham, sleep with his wife's slave girl in order to sire a child. The moral code at that time permitted decisions such as these, and this behavior was not considered infidelity, nor were its products considered illegitimate. However, Isaac chose not to follow this path to fatherhood. Rather:

> *Because Rebekah had no children, Isaac prayed to the Lord for her. The Lord answered his prayer, and Rebekah became pregnant. (Genesis 25:21)*

As much as Isaac longed to have children, he wanted to have them with Rebekah rather than any surrogate, and he was primarily concerned that Rebekah be fulfilled as a woman and mother. Choosing another woman to bear his children would have been humiliating for Rebekah—and make her feel like an absolute failure. Hence, Isaac's prayer to the Lord on her behalf.

As much as Rebekah was undoubtedly thrilled with her pregnancy, some things never come easy. Her pregnancy resulted in a great deal of anguish and physical pain. Yet it was the circumstance of her pregnancy that led the Talmudic rabbis to view her as an authentic prophetess.

> *She was going to have twins, and before they were born, they struggled against each other in her womb. She said, "Why should something like this happen to me?" So she went to ask the Lord for an answer.*
>
> *The Lord said to her, "Two nations are within you; you will give birth to two rival peoples. One will be stronger than the other; the older will serve the younger." (Genesis 25:22-23)*

It was this conversation between Rebekah and the Lord, as well as the Lord's willingness to give Rebekah a glimpse into the future, that led to her designation by the Talmudic scholars as a prophetess. But how Rebekah handled this information has been the subject of both debate and conflicting interpretations.

> *The time came for her to give birth, and she had twin sons. The first one was reddish, and his skin was like a hairy robe, so he was named Esau [which sounds like the Hebrew word for "hairy"]. The second one was born holding on tightly to the heel of Esau, so he was named Jacob [which sounds like the Hebrew word for "heel"]. (Genesis 25:24-26)*

Now Rebekah already knew by the time her sons were born that they would be in some sort of conflict as they grew up—and that Jacob (the younger—even by only a few minutes) would prevail over his elder brother Esau. The Bible offers no clue as to whether Rebekah shared the divine revelation she received while pregnant with her husband Isaac, or whether she kept God's message to herself. Rebekah and Isaac had a very close and loving relationship, so the presumption would be that she shared this revelation with him. But there is no record of this, one way or the other. The Bible does say that:

> The boys grew up. And Esau became a skilled hunter, a man who loved the outdoors, but Jacob was a quiet man who stayed at home. Isaac preferred Esau, because he enjoyed eating the animals Esau killed, but Rebekah preferred Jacob. (Genesis 25:27-28)

THE ISSUE OF BIRTHRIGHT

Even casual readers of the Old Testament are aware of the next story, which may or may not be related to Isaac's upcoming primogenitary blessing. Esau returned home, famished after his long day in the field, while Jacob had remained home, preparing a stew of beans. Their conversation evolved into a negotiation of status in the family:

> Esau...said to Jacob, "I'm starving; give me some of that red stuff [the stew]." Jacob answered, I will give it to you if you give me your rights as the first-born son." Esau said, "All right! I am about to die; what good will my rights do me?"
>
> Jacob answered, "First make a vow that you will give me your rights." Esau made the vow and gave his rights to Jacob. Then Jacob gave him some bread and some of the soup. He ate and drank and then got up and left. That was all Esau cared about his rights as the first-born son." (Genesis 25:29-34)

The covenant made between Abraham and Yahweh was designed to be passed down through each generation of first-born sons, meaning that the original covenant was inherited by Isaac from Abraham, and should have then been likewise been passed down to Esau, whose birth preceded that of Jacob. Esau should have been aware of this responsibility, but has been portrayed as a man with little regard for matters of faith and spirituality, while the opposite has been said of Jacob—that he was a quiet, introspective, faith-filled man of moral integrity. Esau's willingness to trade his birthright would suggest his lack of interest—if not his utter disdain—for the spiritual and moral responsibilities that accompany his status as first-born son. The other possibility—that he was unaware of these responsibilities, that they had never been properly presented to him—would then indict Isaac for a failure to adequately inform and prepare Esau for his future role in the ongoing passage of the Covenant from one generation to the next.

This raises another issue. If Rebekah knew from God before the birth of their twins that the younger (Jacob) would eclipse the elder (Esau), and Rebekah shared this revelation with Isaac, would they have mutually agreed NOT to reveal to Esau the Covenant responsibilities that accompanied his first-born status because they had inferred that his primogeniture would be usurped by Jacob? If so, that might explain why Esau was so quick to barter his birthright for a bowl of soup—he was unaware of its central placement in the Covenant, and, consequently, in salvation history.

Years passed. Eventually Esau married 2 Hittite women—Judith, the daughter of Beeri, and Basemath, the daughter of Elon. The details are unrecorded in Scripture, except for one cryptic passage:

They made life miserable for Isaac and Rebekah. (Genesis 26:35)

THE PRIMOGENITARY BLESSING

Eventually, the now elderly Isaac, who had lost his sight, realized the time had come to bestow his special primogenitary blessing on his first-born son. He asked Esau to kill game and prepare a meal for him, after which he would bestow his blessing. In the world in which Isaac and Esau lived, such a blessing as this one—a father's blessing to his first-born son—carried more weight than a duly signed legal document would have in our own world of today. Above and beyond that, it was thought at the time that the words of the blessing, since they invoked God and were uttered with authority flowing from the Lord, were actually able to bring into reality the blessings they intoned. So the blessing meant a great deal.

Rebekah overheard Isaac's conversation with Esau and his request that Esau prepare a meal prior to the final blessing. It is at this point that Rebekah's actions are open to several different interpretations. The Bible reports that:

> *When Esau went out to hunt, she said to Jacob, "I have just heard your father say to Esau, 'Bring me an animal and cook it for me. After I have eaten it, I will give you my blessing in the presence of the Lord before I die.' Now, son," Rebekah continued, "Listen to me and do what I say. Go to the flock and pick out two fat young goats, so that I can cook them and make some of that food your father likes so much. You can take it to him to eat, and he will give you his blessing before he dies." (Genesis 27:6-10)*

Jacob was rather reticent about this plan, and questioned its viability. He wasn't convinced a substitute meal, in and of itself, would accomplish the objective. Jacob responded:

> *You know that Esau is a hairy man, but I have smooth skin. Perhaps my father will touch me and find out that I am deceiving him; in this way, I will bring a curse on myself instead of a blessing." (Genesis 27:11-12)*

Rebekah, however, had thought ahead—and had planned for such a contingency. She was determined that Jacob, rather than Esau, should be the recipient of this blessing, so she replied:

> *"Let any curse against you fall on me, my son; just do as I say, and go and get the goats for me." (Genesis 27:13)*

Jacob did as she asked him to do. Rebekah cooked the meal, and then placed some of Esau's best clothing on Jacob, putting goatskins on his arms and neck to simulate Esau's hirsutism. Jacob approached his father Isaac, but their conversation revealed some suspicion on the part of Isaac as well as additional lies flowing from the mouth of Jacob, as indicated by this partial digest from Genesis 27:18-27:

> Isaac: *Which of my sons are you?*
>
> Jacob: *I am your older son Esau...Please eat some of the meat I have brought you...*
>
> Isaac: *How did you find it so quickly, son?*
>
> Jacob: *The Lord your God helped me find it.*

Isaac: *Please come closer so I can touch you...Your voice sounds like Jacob's voice, but your arms feel like Esau's arms. Are you really Esau?*

Jacob: *I am.*

Isaac: *Come closer and kiss me, son...The pleasant smell of my son is like the smell of a field which the Lord has blessed.*

Despite Isaac's blindness, he was clearly not easily fooled by this deception. Jacob had to defraud him in terms of time, voice, physicality and smell before Isaac was convinced. It was only after Jacob was able to pass these four "tests" that Isaac was prepared to intone his blessing:

May God give you dew from heaven and make your fields fertile! May he give you plenty of grain and wine! May nations be your servants, and may peoples bow down before you. May you rule over all your relatives. And may your mother's descendants bow down before you. May those who curse you be cursed, and may those who bless you be blessed. (Genesis 27:28-29).

As soon as Jacob had received the blessing, Esau returned from his hunting expedition, prepared a meal and brought it to Isaac. When Esau discovered Jacob's deception, he was distraught and furious, demanding that Isaac bless him as well. Isaac's response was uncompromising:

I gave him my final blessing, and so it is his forever...Your brother came and deceived me. He has taken away your blessing...I have already made him master over you. And I have made all his relatives his slaves. I have given him grain and wine. Now there is nothing that I can do for you, son. (Genesis 27:33-37)

At this point Esau blamed Jacob from stealing his birthright and his blessing, He may have had a valid claim about his primogenitary blessing, but he was responsible himself for trading away his birthright. Regardless of the validity of his accusations, he was determined to kill Jacob as soon as Isaac had passed away. When Rebekah discovered these plans of Esau, she was determined, of course, to thwart them. She told Jacob:

Listen, your brother Esau is planning to get even with you and kill you. Now, son, do what I say. Go at once to my brother Laban in Haran, and stay with him for awhile, until your brother's anger cools down and he forgets what you have done to him. Then I will send someone to bring you back. (Genesis 27:42-45)

Rebekah also complained to Isaac about Esau's two Hittite wives, and how she wouldn't want Jacob to follow the same path. So Isaac echoed Rebekah's idea that Jacob should travel to Mesopotamia, when he told Jacob:

Don't marry a Canaanite girl. Go instead to Mesopotamia, to the home of your grandfather Bethuel, and marry one of the girls there, one of your uncle Laban's daughters. May Almighty God bless your marriage and give you many children, so that you will become the father of many nations! May He bless you and your descendants as he blessed Abraham, and may you take possession of this land, in which you have lived and which God gave to Abraham. (Genesis 28:1-5)

DIFFERING VIEWS ON REBEKAH

For all intents and purposes, this departure of Jacob to Haran to escape his brother's wrath and to secure himself a bride—even though there is still much to report about *his* future and the passage of the Covenant to the next generation—ends the story of Rebekah, and it ends on a rather empty and desolate note for her. If the Bible is accurate in reporting that Rebekah truly and deeply favored Jacob over Esau, then it is quite sad that she never saw him again, despite her promise to send someone to bring him back "when the coast was clear." Jacob remained in Haran for twenty years, never returning to Canaan before Rebekah's death.

How should Rebekah and the decisions she made be viewed in hindsight? As said earlier, she has been the subject of both praise and criticism by Biblical scholars, who offer contradictory analyses of her behavior. On the negative side, Rebekah's critics condemn her for her display of obvious favoritism of one son over the other. Aren't parents supposed to treat and love all of their children equally? She has been condemned, after apparently loving her husband Isaac for so many years, for deliberately taking advantage of his infirmities to deceive him and use a clever ruse to thwart his dying wish and secure his final blessing for one who was not entitled to receive it.

Other critics of Rebekah will argue that Isaac was aware of Esau's spiritual and moral deficiencies, but was confident that his final blessing, if properly bestowed on Esau, would help to transform him in some way—with God's help—into a worthy recipient of his Covenant responsibilities and patriarchal status.

Still others argue that Rebekah's faith in God was too shallow—that if God had told her while pregnant that her younger son would prevail over his older brother, she should have trusted that God would and could see it to fruition. Her intervention was, therefore, unnecessary and unwarranted.

Rebekah's advocates paint an entirely different picture. They see Rebekah as a courageous young woman who was willing to give up the life she knew in Haran to venture into the unknown—marriage to a man she had never met and life in a country (Canaan) of which she knew nothing. They point out that she did this based on her faith that this match was ordained by God, suggesting that her faith was anything but shallow. When she became pregnant after twenty years of marriage, experiencing great prenatal anguish, God gifted her with a glimpse into the future lives and destinies of her two sons. They maintain that she must have confided this to Isaac, who was well aware that Jacob would ultimately triumph over Esau, and that when that triumph seemed threatened, she acted proactively to preserve God's plans.

Defenders of Rebekah also point out that there is no evidence of Isaac issuing a reprimand or censure of Jacob for disguising himself as Esau to secure Isaac's blessing. One would expect that such a deception would induce anger and embarrassment on Isaac's part. Rather, Isaac agreed with Rebekah that Jacob should journey to Mesopotamia in search of a wife, and even blessed him and his descendants before Jacob departed. These are not the words and actions of one who has been played as a fool.

Rebekah's supporters view her as a woman of action, as a contrast to Isaac, who they consider much more of an introspective milquetoast. Some have even claimed that a roster of the Patriarchs of the Chosen People should not read "Abraham, Isaac, Jacob and Joseph," but rather "Abraham, Rebekah, Jacob and Joseph." It seems as if the Talmudic scholars who view Rebekah as an authentic prophet are more likely to fall into this second category.

QUESTIONS FOR REVIEW

1. How did Abraham's servant hope to find the right spouse for Isaac?

2. What was the justification for the Talmudic rabbis to consider Rebekah to be a prophetess?

3. What did God reveal to Rebekah about the future of her two twins?

4. In what ways can Jacob and Esau be contrasted? Do they share any common characteristics?

5. Did Jacob "trick" Esau into surrendering his birthright? Explain your reasoning.

6. What role did Rebekah play in Isaac's primogenitary blessing?

7. Can you justify the description of Rebekah as manipulative and deceptive?

8. Can you justify Rebekah as a woman of great faith and action?

Chapter Thirteen
RAHAB

After Moses successfully led the Chosen People out of their bondage in Egypt in the Exodus event, Moses and his followers wandered throughout the Sinai Desert for a period of forty years. Early in their desert sojourn, upon reaching Mount Sinai, Moses had a personal audience on the hilltop with the Lord, Who gifted Moses with the Ten Commandments. It was at this point that these Israelites committed themselves to the Lord and were baptized in blood by Moses. The reception of the Ten Commandments (or *Decalogue*, as they were called in Greek) was a watershed moment in Israelite history as the event that united them as a people, and is celebrated annually as the "birthday" of Judaism at the spring feast of Shavuot.

Moses, in leading his people out of Egypt, was hoping to return them to the land of Canaan—the land initially given by God to

Abraham but vacated by Abraham's descendants when Joseph, Abraham's great-grandson, invited his family to join him in Egypt after he had risen to great prominence in that country. That, of course, was several hundred years before the tide of popular opinion turned against them and the Israelites were subsequently enslaved by the Egyptians.

While Moses' campaign to lead the Israelites out of Egyptian slavery was eminently successful, he fell short of accomplishing his ultimate goal of returning his people to Canaan. Moses died before crossing the River Jordan into his ancestral homeland, and the task of leading the people into Canaan then fell to his lieutenant and successor, Joshua, the son of Nun.

JOSHUA'S GREAT TASK

God made it very clear to Joshua what he was expected to do when He said:

My servant Moses is dead. Get ready now, you and all the people of Israel, and cross the Jordan River into the land that I am giving them. As I told Moses, I have given you and all My people the entire land that you will be marching over. Your borders will reach from the desert in the south to the Lebanon Mountains in the north; from the great Euphrates River in the east, through the Hittite country, to the Mediterranean Sea in the west. Joshua, no one will be able to defeat you as long as you live. I will be with you as I was with Moses. I will always be with you; I will never abandon you. Be determined and confident, for you will be the leader of these people as they occupy this land which I promised their ancestors. Just be determined, be confident; and be sure you obey the whole Law that My servant Moses gave you. Do not neglect any part of it and you will succeed wherever you go. (Joshua 1:2-7)

Joshua had been given his instructions from the Lord, and he began to organize the Israelites for their upcoming excursion into Canaan. Included among the many decisions he needed to make was his desire to learn more about the land of Canaan he and his followers were about to invade. So Joshua opted to send two scouts, or spies, to go on ahead, explore the land, and report back to him. One of the sites they needed to investigate was the heavily fortified, walled city of Jericho which lay directly in the path ahead of them.

It's unclear if Joshua were aware of this at the time—probably not—but the people of Jericho were already cognizant of the Israelite departure from Egypt as well as the great power of their God in leading them through the Red Sea as He vanquished the pursuing Egyptian army. So the people of Jericho, realizing that the Israelites were heading in their direction, were nothing less than terrified at their approach. And this terror overwhelmed them despite the incredibly heavy fortifications that would make it very difficult for an enemy to overpower them. Jericho was protected by two walls that completely encircled the city—one that was six feet thick and a second that was twelve feet thick. And this is the circumstance that led to Rahab.

The two spies sent to Jericho by Joshua—Caleb and Phinehas—travelled around the city, taking stock of its layout and defenses, points of entry and egress, etc. Ultimately they found themselves at the establishment owned and operated by Rahab. What kind of establishment was it? What kind of person was Rahab? Two excellent questions with contrary answers for each.

RAHAB'S QUESTIONABLE DECISIONS

Before considering Rahab, it should be noted that she is usually *not* included in most of the listings of the prophetesses of the Old Testament, except on rare occasions. In Pope Clement I's *First Epistle to the Corinthians*, written circa 96 CE, in referring to Rahab, Clement wrote, 'You see, loved ones, not only was faith found in the woman, but prophecy as well." Other random references to Rahab as a prophetess have been made by others as well—but they are, frankly, few and far between.

Rahab has been described as one of the most beautiful women who ever lived. The Talmudic rabbis equate her beauty with that of Sarah (Abraham's wife), Rebekah (Isaac's wife), Abigail (David's wife) and Esther (King Xerxes' wife). It has been said about Rahab that just the mention of her name would drive men into lustful fits and seminal emissions. Rahab is almost universally described as a prostitute, a harlot—not one of the cultic prostitutes who "performs" as part of an idolatrous religious rite, but a street prostitute who "plies her wares" for money. As such, she was viewed as a woman of very low moral standards—an abject sinner. On a kinder, if not necessarily more accurate note, Rahab has also been labeled as an innkeeper. It was not uncommon in Canaan during this time period for lodging establishments such as a wayfarer's inn to double as a brothel. So Rahab, in reality, was probably both a prostitute and an innkeeper.

The circumstances that led to the arrival of Caleb and Phinehas at Rahab's residence is unclear, but they spent the night at her establishment, which was located adjacent to the outer wall of the city. Through sources of his own, the king of Jericho was made aware of the two Israelites in his city and knew that they had found their way to Rahab's. So he sent some members of his court to arrest them and bring them before him, most probably for interrogation and possible execution. Rahab was told:

> *The men in your house have come to spy out the whole country! Bring them out! (Joshua 2:3)*

Rahab had already decided to hide the Israelite spies rather than surrender them to the king, so she hid them on the roof of her house under a pile of flax and told the king's agents:

> *Some men did come to my house...but I don't know where they were from.*
>
> *They left at sundown before the city gate was closed. I didn't find out where they were going, but if you start out quickly after them, you can catch them. (Joshua 2:4-5)*

With the king's men now diverted and preoccupied, Rahab was able to explain her actions to the enemy spies for whom she had just lied and committed treason, while at the same time striking a deal to the advantage of her family:

> *I know that the Lord [Yahweh] has given you this land. Everyone in the country is terrified of you. We have heard how the Lord dried up the Red Sea in front of you when you were leaving Egypt. We have also heard how you killed Sihon and Og, the two Amorite kings east of the Jordan. We were afraid as soon as we heard about it; we have all lost our courage because of you.*
>
> *The Lord your God is God in heaven above and here on earth. Now swear by Him that you will treat my family as kindly as I have treated you, and give me some sign that I can trust you. Promise me that you will save my father and mother, my brothers and sisters, and all their families! Don't let us be killed! (Joshua 2:9-13)*

Caleb and Phinehas agreed to make arrangements to spare and protect Rahab and her family once Jericho had been conquered. Rahab lowered the men down a rope from a window on the outer wall of the city fortifications and instructed them to hide in the nearby hill country away from the direction she sent the king's agents. They, in turn, told her to hang a red cord from the window in which she lowered them to show the Israelite troops which house to spare. This rope is reminiscent of the red blood of the lambs that dripped from the Israelite dwellings in Egypt on the night of Passover, when the inhabitants were also spared from death and destruction. Christians see the red cord as symbolic of the blood of Christ. Rahab was to see to it that all the members of her family were within that home at the time of the conquest of Jericho.

CONVERSION AND TRANSFORMATION

While it is indisputable that Rahab was an exceedingly brave woman to betray her king in shielding Caleb and Phinehas and consequently supporting an Israelite attack on Jericho, it is equally true—and quite amazing—that she had developed a deep faith in Yahweh, a God foreign to her neighbors in Jericho as well as to the other tribes living throughout Canaan. And it was this faith in Yahweh that convinced her that the Israelites had a legitimate claim on the land of Canaan, that it was the will of Yahweh that His Chosen People should occupy the land, that He would help them to achieve this, and that the Israelites would emerge victorious in their attack. It is for these reasons that some view Rahab as an authentic prophetess. Their thought process is as follows: as a Canaanite woman who grew up without any exposure to the Israelites and their God, the only way she could have developed such strong convictions about the power of Yahweh and the destined victory of the Israelites would be if Yahweh has personally revealed Himself to her and informed her of the happenings about to unfold. That would make Rahab a woman who had been given a specific message from God which she, in turn, shared with Caleb and Phinehas, both in hiding them and in making a deal with them to protect her family. And that is the accepted definition of a prophet—one who receives a message from the Lord and delivers it, as the Lord has commanded. In her 2009 monograph entitled "Rahab: Bible," Dr. Tikva Frymer-Kensky of the University of Chicago Divinity School described Rahab as one who "begins as triple marginalized—Canaanite, woman and prostitute" but who "moves to the center as bearer of a divine message and herald of Israel in its new land." Shannon Martin of the C.S. Lewis Institute echoed these sentiments when she asked, "Now how on earth would a pagan woman, who is lowly and poor with a horrible job, not only learn about the God of Israel, but also come to such an absolute faith in him as her God as well? Divine revelation is the answer." These sentiments certainly make a case for considering Rahab to be a prophetess.

When the Israelites conquered Jericho and utterly laid waste to it, they rescued, as promised, Rahab and her family, who were taken safely to the Israelite camp. This might be where the story of Rahab would probably come to its end, but that is far from the case. Rahab is not mentioned further in the Book of Joshua, appearing only in chapters 2 and 6. But despite the absence of written Scriptural documentation, it would seem that Rahab's contributions to salvation history have not yet come to an end. Judaic tradition maintains that Rahab transformed herself into a pillar of faith and service within the Israelite community, which welcomed her into its ranks. Although in some places it is inferred that Rahab eventually married Joshua, there is no Biblical evidence to support that Joshua ever took a wife, much less Rahab. The prevailing opinion is that Rahab married Salmon, and they had a son named Boaz.

There is little specific information on record about Salmon, except that he was the son of Nahshon, who was a chieftain in the tribe of Judah. Boaz, their son, went on to become a wealthy landowner in the town of Bethlehem, where he met and married Ruth. While no further mention is made of Rahab throughout the rest of the Hebrew Scriptures, the Book of Ruth details the life story of the Moabite woman Ruth and her subsequent marriage to Boaz.

The importance of Rahab's marriage to Salmon and the birth of their son Boaz may seem relatively (pardon the pun!) unimportant—but that conclusion would be erroneous. While Rahab's name appears nowhere else in the Old Testament, it *does* appear in the New Testament. As a matter of fact, Rahab's name almost opens the New Testament, when she is mentioned in the first chapter of the Gospel of Matthew:

> *This is the list of the ancestors of Jesus Christ, a descendant of David, who was a descendant of Abraham.*
>
> *From Abraham to King David, the following ancestors are listed: Abraham, Isaac, Jacob, Judah and his brothers; then Perez and Zerah (their mother was Tamar), Hezron, Ram, Amminadab, Nahshon, Salmon, Boaz (his mother was Rahab), Obed (his mother was Ruth), Jesse and King David.*
>
> *From David to the time when the people of Israel were taken into exile in Babylon, the following ancestors are listed: David, Solomon (his mother [Bathsheba] was the woman who had been Uriah's wife), Rehoboam, Abijah, Asa, Jehoshaphat, Jehoram, Uzziah, Jotham, Ahaz, Hezekiah, Manasseh, Amon, Josiah, and Jehoiachin and his brothers.*
>
> *From the time after the exile in Babylon to the birth of Jesus, the following ancestors are listed: Jehoiachin, Shealtiel, Zerubbabel, Abiud, Eliakim, Azor, Zadok, Achim, Eliud, Eleazar, Matthan, Jacob, and Joseph, who married Mary, the mother of Jesus, Who was called the Messiah.*

> *So then, there were fourteen generations from Abraham to David, and fourteen from David to the exile in Babylon, and fourteen from then to the birth of the Messiah. (Matthew 1:1-17)*

Rahab started out life essentially (since she was a Canaanite) as an enemy of Israel. On top of that, as a prostitute, she was considered a person of reprehensible, immoral conduct—someone who lived very much on the outskirts of her own home town of Jericho—literally and figuratively, since her home abutted the outer wall of the city. And as a woman, she would have had very little power to improve her status.

Yet, there's another side to Rahab that speaks of both transformation and redemption. She came to believe in Yahweh and His power as well as the rightful place of the Israelites as the true landholders and rulers of Canaan. She bravely rejected the gods of Canaan, lied to her own king and sent his representatives on a wild goose chase to protect the Israelite spies residing with her. She bargained with these spies not only to protect herself, but to safeguard her extended family as well. And while prostitution, false witness and treason aren't usually the actions we connect with heroism, Rahab used quick wits, love and deep faith to propel the Israelites into a resounding victory in Jericho and protect her own loved ones in the process. It may not be an exaggeration to say that her actions may have changed the wartime tide in favor of the Israelites. And after she was accepted into the Israelite fold, she emerged as a woman of righteousness and faith—a transformation so complete that she was granted the divine privilege of emerging as a blood ancestor to the generation of forthcoming Israelite kings—and ultimately an ancestor of Jesus, the promised Messiah.

Was Rahab really a prophetess? The jury is out; history is still indecisive. There is evidence to say "yes" and evidence to say "no." But even if the answer is ultimately in the negative, Rahab is the proverbial "silk purse that emerged from the sow's ear" and a role model of redemption and transformation.

QUESTIONS FOR REVIEW

1. What task was entrusted by God to Joshua?

2. How did Joshua hope to prepare for an attack on Jericho?

3. What was Rahab's occupation?

4. Why did Rahab choose to provide assistance to the Israelite spies?

5. How did Rahab deal with her king's representatives?

6. What was the nature of the deal Rahab made with the two spies?

7. Why do some view Rahab as a prophetess while others do not?

8. What was Rahab's "transformation?"

9. Why is Rahab mentioned by name in the Gospel of St. Matthew?

Chapter Fourteen

SAMSON'S MOTHER, THE WIFE OF MANOAH

The Bible is replete with colorful characters and personalities from whom we learn lessons of faith, love, courage, humility and devotion to God. Samson, the Nazirite judge of Israel who led Israel during a twenty-year period when the Israelites were under Philistine domination, is one such character. Even casual readers of the Bible are aware of Samson's superhuman strength and his betrayal by his wife Delilah, whose name, even in this day and age over three thousand years later, is associated with treachery. But how many are equally familiar with Samson's mother—and why should they be?

Samson's mother only appears in the Old Testament in Chapters 13 and 14 of the Book of Judges. Like Rebekah and Rahab, she is not listed among the prophetesses of the Hebrew Scriptures, yet there are those who make a case for her inclusion. Is their case warranted?

While the Bible does not mention her by name, Dr. Tamar Kadari of the Schechter Institute of Jewish Studies pointed out in a 2009 monograph entitled "Wife of Manoah; Samson's Mother: Midrash and Aggadah" that "the Babylonian rabbis knew Manoah's wife as 'Zlelponi' or 'Zlelponith'...a name that affiliates her with the tribe of Judah." Dr. Kadari went on to explain that her husband "Manoah was from Zorah, from a Danite family...The Rabbis deduce from this that Samson's father was from the tribe of Dan, while his mother was of Judahite descent, thereby associating Samson, who judged Israel for twenty years, with the Israelite royal tribe."

Like many other women in the Bible (Sarah, Rebecca, Hannah, etc.) who were forced—usually over a protracted period of time—to deal with their sterility and feel the terrible reality that motherhood would forever be outside their grasp, Samson's mother faced this same issue. But her outlook and her entire world changed on one historic day:

> The Lord's angel appeared to her and said, "You have never been able to have children, but you will soon be pregnant and have a son. Be sure not to drink any wine or beer, or eat any forbidden food; and after your son is born, you must never cut his hair, because from the day of his birth he will be dedicated to God as a Nazirite. He will begin the work of rescuing Israel from the Philistines." (Judges 13:3-5)

Nazirites were persons (men or women) who were pledged to God—sometimes perpetually and other times for designated periods of time—by maintaining a constant state of ritual purity. The word "nazirite" comes from the Hebrew word *nazir*, meaning "consecrated" or "set apart." They observed this by abstaining from products of the vine and all forbidden foods and by avoiding both corpses and gravesites. For the men, refusing to cut one's hair was an outward sign of this commitment to God, the opposite of medieval monks whose hair was tonsured (shaven from the crown of the head) as a physical sign of their dedication to God. In the case of Samson, who was called to Nazirite life even prior to his mother's conception of him, she was required also to abstain from alcohol and forbidden foods while Samson was in utero.

Zlelponi (if that is indeed her name) was unaware that she had been visited by an angel, believing him to be a prophet, although she admitted to her husband Manoah that:

> ...he looked as frightening as an angel of God. I didn't ask him where he came from, and he didn't tell me his name. (Judges 13:6)

Whether Manoah didn't believe his wife or was unsure how to deal with the situation should it happen to be true, he prayed to the Lord to send the "man of God" back to them for further instructions. Manoah wanted to see this "man of God" for himself. God sent the angel back a second time, but again, only to Zlelponi when she was by herself, sitting in the field. Upon his arrival, Zlelponi retrieved Manoah, to whom the angel repeated most of what he had previously mentioned to his wife. After Manoah asked the angel for his name (which the angel did not give), and invited the angel to stay and dine (which the angel did not do), Manoah sacrificed both a goat and some grain on an altar to the Lord.

While the flames were going up from the altar, Manoah and his wife saw the Lord's angel go up toward heaven in the flames. Manoah realized then that the man had been the Lord's angel, and he and his wife threw themselves face downward on the ground. They never saw the angel again.

Manoah said to his wife, "We are sure to die, because we have seen God!" But his wife answered, "If the Lord had wanted to kill us, he would not have accepted our offerings; He would not have shown us all this or told us such things at this time." (Judges 13:20-23)

Do the events in Zlelponi's life qualify her to be listed among the prophets? From the Book of Judges we can accurately deduce that she was a deeply faithful and spiritual woman whose devotion to God was beyond reproach. Not only was she granted the gift she so desperately wanted—a child—but she was visited by a divine messenger who informed her of God's gift and entrusted her with special responsibilities not only for her son, but for herself as well. We are also able to discern that she was a woman of both insight and intelligence. She suspected that there was more to the "man of God" than met the eye, and she realized when she and Manoah witnessed the ascension of the angel, he was an angel (not GOD Himself!), so her husband's fear of death was absurd, given the news they had received of their impending parenthood. Dr. Kadari pointed out that, in the eyes of the Babylonian Talmudic rabbis, "Manoah was an ignoramus who did not even learn Scripture, while his wife was a righteous woman."

Perhaps the opinion of those who do believe that Manoah's wife is worthy of consideration as a prophetess is summed up most succinctly by Dr. Christine Marchetti, professor of Sacred Scripture at Holy Apostles College in Connecticut, who pointed out quite clearly and simply in the *Priscilla Papers*, the academic journal of CBE International, in 2018, "Samson's mother (known only as the wife of Manoah) received a divine message concerning her pregnancy; she alone (not her husband) was able to interpret it." Again, are not messages from God and the presentation of them to others the characteristics of a prophetess?

QUESTIONS FOR REVIEW

1. Is Samson's mother's name recorded in the Book of Judges? Do we know what it is?

2. How was she made aware that she would become pregnant?

3. What special instructions accompanied her pregnancy?

4. What is a Nazirite?

5. What was her husband's reaction to her pregnancy?

6. On what grounds do some consider her a prophetess?

Chapter Fifteen
QUEEN MOTHER OF LEMUEL

Another one of the more questionable prophetesses of the Old Testament is a woman who was quoted by her son in one chapter of one book of the Hebrew Scriptures—chapter 31 of the Book of Proverbs. What makes her designation as a prophetess a debatable one is the fact that Biblical scholars are unaware of her identity, if she really existed or if she exists merely as a fictional character. A little bit of background information is in order.

It is generally accepted as fact that most of the Book of Proverbs was composed by King Solomon. Given the fact that Solomon was renowned for his wisdom and the Book of Solomon is replete with sayings and bon mots that offered bits of wisdom covering a wide range of both spiritual and secular matters, this makes a great deal of sense. Proverbs consists of 31 chapters, and Solomon is given credit for the composition—or at least the inspiration—for the first 29 chapters. The opening line of chapter 30 reveals its author to be Agur, son of Jakeh, about whom nothing else is really known. Some scholars believe that Agur may be another designation for Solomon, but there is no further evidence one way or the other.

Chapter 31, the last chapter of Proverbs, is ascribed to the mother of King Lemuel—words that were meaningful enough to Lemuel to remember, to write down and to pass along to others. The question arises, who is King Lemuel? In the annals of Jewish history, there is no mention of a monarch named Lemuel, even when the Chosen People split into two separate nations after the death of King Solomon—even though this section of Proverbs is thought to have been written long before that era. So again, Biblical scholars are left in a quandary. It is thought by some scholars that Lemuel, like Agur, may be just another name for Solomon. If that is true, and the words of chapter 31 are indeed inspired by his mother, then we also know that their originator would have to be Bathsheba, the mother of Solomon—the Bathsheba whose tryst with David ultimately led to many, many interpersonal familial problems and a great deal of anguish, even though David and Bathsheba eventually married, and David was succeeded as king by their son Solomon. Still, the actual identity of Lemuel is uncertain, and the possibility that he might actually be a nom de plume for Solomon is unsubstantiated. Some scholars also posit that Lemuel may be the king of a nation known as Massa, possibly located somewhere in northern Africa.

Chapter 31 consists of 31 verses, the first nine of which, inspired by Lemuel's mother, offer advice to her royal son:

You are my own dear son, the answer to my prayers. What shall I tell you?

Don't spend all your energy on sex and all your money on women; they have destroyed kings. Listen, Lemuel. Kings should not drink wine or have a craving for alcohol. When they drink, they forget the laws and ignore the rights of people in need. Alcohol is for people who are dying, for those who are in misery. Let them drink and forget their poverty and unhappiness.

Speak up for people who cannot speak for themselves. Protect the rights of all who are helpless. Speak for them and be a righteous judge. Protect the rights of the poor and needy. (Proverbs 1:2-9)

The remaining verses in this chapter describe the qualities and attributes of a virtuous or ideal wife. Again, the debate goes on as to the identity of the author of this section of Chapter 31. Is it also inspired by the Queen Mother of Lemuel—or was it added later, composed by a different writer? If the previous lines in Chapter 31 encourage Lemuel not to be too preoccupied with matters of the flesh, such as women and wine, then a codicil explaining the kind of woman who would complement a king seems like an appropriate segue. What leads some to view verses 10-31 as composed by another author is the difference in writing style: verses 10-31 (22 lines long) are written in an acrostic style—each verse beginning with the next letter in the 22-character Hebrew alphabet. Of course, this style does not reveal itself in the following English translation:

How hard it is to find a capable wife! She is worth far more than pearls!

Her husband puts his confidence in her, and he will never be poor.

As long as she lives, she does him good and never harm.

She keeps herself busy making wool and linen cloth.

She brings home food from out-of-the-way places, as merchant ships do.

She gets up before daylight to prepare food for her family and to tell her servant girls what to do.

She looks at land and buys it, and with money she has earned, she plants a vineyard.

She is a hard worker, strong and industrious.

She knows the value of everything she makes, and works late into the night.

She spins her own thread and weaves her own cloth.

She is generous to the poor and needy.

She doesn't worry when it snows, because her family has warm clothing.

She makes bedspreads and wears clothes of fine purple linen.

Her husband is well known, one of the leading citizens.

She makes clothes and belts, and sells them to merchants.

She is strong and respected and not afraid of the future.

She speaks with a gentle wisdom.

She is always busy and looks after her family's needs.

Her children show their appreciation, and her husband praises her.

He says, "Many women are good wives, but you are the best of them all."

Charm is deceptive and beauty disappears, but a woman who honors the Lord should be praised.

Give her credit for all she does. She deserves the respect of everyone. (Proverbs 31:10-31)

Again, this second section of chapter 31 may have been composed at a different time by a different author and added to chapter 31 at a much later date. But it is included here because it may very well conclude the material ascribed by King Lemuel to his mother.

Like a connect-the-dots drawing, a number of "ifs" must be lined up properly to consider the Queen Mother of Lemuel to be a prophetess. IF she is real person (not a character of fiction) and IF her son is also a real person and IF she expressed these thoughts to him as advice to guide his royal efforts and IF he was so enamored with them that he remembered them, wrote them down, and passed them along to others, and IF these words of the Queen Mother were indeed inspired by God to be passed along to a wider audience, THEN, perhaps, the Queen Mother of Lemuel can rightly be accorded the status of prophetess.

Pastor David Guzik, the former director and professor at Calvary Chapel Bible College, pointed out that, "Like Solomon and Agur, Lemuel understood that his words were an utterance, a prophecy or revelation, from God which his mother taught him: Perhaps like Timothy (2 Timothy 1:5) Lemuel had a Jewish mother who taught him the fear of the LORD and God's wisdom."

While the Good News Bible, which is used throughout this text for its contemporary translation of Scripture does not use the word "inspired" or "prophetic" in its description of the Queen Mother's words to Lemuel, a number of other contemporary translations do. The New International Version calls her words "an inspired utterance," the King James Bible calls them "a prophecy," and God's Word Translation hails them as "a prophetic revelation." The importance of words such as "inspired" and "prophetic" cannot be underestimated, because their presence draws a direct connection between God (as the source of the revelation) and the person who proclaims it on His behalf (the messenger who delivers it to a larger and wider audience.) In other words...a prophet(ess). St. Peter's Second Epistle very clearly states that,

"...no prophetic message ever came...but...under the control of the Holy Spirit...as [a] message from God." (2 Peter 1:21)

QUESTIONS FOR REVIEW

I. Why is the identity of King Lemuel problematic?

2. What does the presence of these words in the Book of Proverbs suggest about the relationship between Lemuel and the Queen Mother?

3. What is the nature of the advice the Queen Mother wishes to pass along to her son?

4. What are the characteristics of an "ideal wife", according to verses 10-31 in chapter 31 of Proverbs?

5. Is the Queen Mother a prophetess? What evidence (if any) supports this position?

Chapter Sixteen
THE FEMALE GUILD PROPHETS

At different times throughout the history of the Old Testament, mention is made of the presence of "guild prophets"—men and women who lived in community under the leadership of a prophetic master from whom they took instruction. Male and female prophetic guilds were separate from one another. These guilds seem to have emerged in the latter days of the period of the judges of Israel all the way through Judaic history to the return of the exiled Judeans to their homeland after the conquest of Babylon by Persia. Prophetic guilds are mentioned in relation to the prophets Samuel, Elisha and Isaiah of Jerusalem, and Amos is a prophet who claimed to be neither a prophet nor a member of one of these guilds.

Perhaps the greatest problem with the presence of these prophetic guilds is that their very existence is based on a misunderstanding of the nature of prophethood itself. Those who joined such guilds did so in the belief that they could be taught to be prophets. Through a variety of techniques such as dancing, singing, self-flagellation, etc. they hoped to advance themselves into an ecstatic state of altered consciousness to induce direct communion with God. This belief in the possibility of choosing prophethood as a career embraced the idea that being a prophet did not necessarily flow from a calling by God. Rather, it could be accomplished through one's own efforts. The prophetic guilds associated with authentic prophets such as Samuel and Elisha had a different function—their members were under instructions not to aspire to become prophets—but to serve as teachers to an Israel and Judah who had fallen away from authentic faith and commitment to Yahweh.

It was to Ezekiel in Babylon that the Lord expressed His frustration at the efforts of these guild prophets, and He ordered Ezekiel to denounce them. At the time, there were separate guilds of men and women. In the case of the women, Dr. Christine Marchetti listed the activities they pursued that incurred God's wrath. "The female prophets are accused of making charms for magic or divination. Apparently they were seen as quite powerful, and charged fees for their services...The language and imagery describing their activities is typical of Mesopotamian anti-witchcraft rituals, and at least two interpretations are possible: (1) They were primitive healthcare practitioners who used charms and incantations to protect women during childbirth and pregnancy, and through divination they predicted whether their patients would live or die. (2) They were necromancers. But Ezekiel's language is not descriptive of any specific practices; it is stereotypical,

THE FEMALE GUILD PROPHETS • 189

reflecting a general, pre-exilic diversity of beliefs and practices..."

To Ezekiel, the Lord issued the following instructions:

> *Now, mortal man, look at the women among your people who make up predictions. Denounce them and tell them what the Sovereign Lord is saying to them: "You women are doomed! You sew magic wristbands for everyone and make magic scarves for everyone to wear on their heads, so that they can have power over other people's lives. You want to possess the power of life and death over My people and to use it for your own benefit.*
>
> *You dishonor Me in front of My people in order to get a few handfuls of barley and a few pieces of bread. You kill people who don't deserve to die, and you keep people alive who don't deserve to live. So you tell lies to My people, and they believe you.*
>
> *...I hate the wristbands that you use in your attempt to control life and death. I will rip them off your arms and set free the people that you were controlling. I will rip off your scarves and let My people escape from your power once and for all. Then you will know that I am the Lord.*
>
> *By your lies you discourage good people, whom I do not wish to hurt.*
>
> *You prevent evil people from giving up evil and saving their lives. So now your false visions and misleading predictions are over. I am rescuing My people from your power, so that you will know that I am the Lord."* (Ezekiel 13:17-23)

Clearly, this final group of women prophets were anything but what they claimed to be. They were *not* spokespersons for the

Lord, and He Himself denounced their intentions and their activities. It should be mentioned in the interest of justice and parity that God was equally displeased with other guilds of false male prophets as well, so Ezekiel had his hands full in condemning the activities of all of these guilds. If the women in these guilds were to be viewed in any way as prophetesses—it would have been as false ones—not as authentic ones!

QUESTIONS FOR REVIEW

1. What were guild prophets?

2. During what time period did they primarily exist?

3. For what reasons did God tell Ezekiel to denounce the female guild prophets?

EPILOGUE

Prophethood is a free gift from God. It is the Lord Who chooses the prophet—and not vice versa. Those who would wish to serve the Lord as authentic prophets and prophetesses may have the best of motivations, and their desire to dedicate themselves to God may be absolutely genuine, but the selection process begins and ends with God Himself. Most of the women mentioned in this text were great and important messengers of the Lord—every bit as significant and noteworthy as their male counterparts. It is an incredible disservice to the countless other women prophets whose messages and ministries have never found their way onto the pages of Sacred Scripture—expunged, most probably, by a patristic and chauvinistic attitude that has unfortunately prevailed throughout the ages—and still exists in a 21st century CE world that claims to be more enlightened, tolerant and unbiased than it has proven itself to be.

Maybe in the years to come, archaeological and paleontological discoveries will uncover long hidden contributions of other women prophets whose words may lead us to a greater and deeper knowledge and appreciation of the ongoing sweep of salvation history. And maybe a more all-inclusive attitude on the part of Biblical scholars and exegetes will offer encouragement to re-double their efforts to explore the contributions of these—and other—Biblical women of stature. Who knows what additional insights and revelations are still out there, just waiting to be discovered?

BIBLIOGRAPHY

Bird, Phyllis Ann. *Missing Persons and Mistaken Identities; Women and Gender in Ancient Israel*. Fortress Press, 1997, Minneapolis MN

Blenkinsopp, Joseph. *A History of Prophecy in Israel*. Westminster John Knox Press, 1983, Louisville KY

Coopersmith, Dina. "Women in the Bible" series. www.aish.com

Camp, Claudia V. *The Encyclopedia of Jewish Women*. Jewish Women's Archive, 1997, Brookline MA

Friedlander, Rachel. "Five Things About Esther That Nobody Talks About." *Issues*. 19 February 2019

Frymer-Kensky, Tikva. "Rahab: Bible." Jewish Women: A Comprehensive Historical Encyclopedia. 27 February 2009. Jewish Women's Archive. https://jwa.org/encyclopedia/article/rahab-bible

Gafney, Wilda C. *Daughters of Miriam: Women Prophets in Ancient Israel*. Fortress Press, 2008, Minneapolis MN

Goodman, Shalom. "Sarah of the Bible: The First Matriarch." www.chabad.org

Greenberg, Blu. "Jewish Divorce Law." *Lilith*. Summer 1977

Guzik, David. "Proverbs 31: The Wisdom of King Solomon" https//:enduringword.com/bible-commentary/proverbs-31, 2020

Henry, Matthew. *Complete Bible Commentary*. 1706

Hieronimus, J. Zohara Meyerhoff. *Kabbalistic Teachings of the Female Prophets: The Seven Holy Women of Ancient Israel*. Inner Traditions, 2008, Rochester VT

Josephus, Flavius. *Antiquities of the Jews*. 93

Kadari, Tamar. *"Hannah: Midrash and Aggadah."* Jewish Women: A Comprehensive Historical Encyclopedia. 20 March 2009. Jewish Women's Archive. https://jwa.org/encyclopedia/article/hannah-midrash-and-aggadah

Kadari, Tamar. *"Wife of Manoah; Samson's Mother: Midrash and Aggadah."* Jewish Women: A Comprehensive Historical Encyclopedia. 27 February 2009. Jewish Women's Archive. https://jwa.org/encyclopedia/article/wife-of-manoah-samsons-mother-midrash-and-aggadah

Kavanagh, Preston. *Huldah: The Prophet Who Wrote Hebrew Scripture*. Pickwick Publications, 2012, Eugene OR (Used by permission of Wipf and Stock Publishers. www.wipfandstock.com)

Kavon, Eli. "The Evil King Manasseh: Idolatry and Politics." Jerusalem Post, 11 July 2016

Mandel, David. *Who's Who in the Jewish Bible*. The Jewish Publication Society, 2014, Philadelphia PA

Marchetti, Christine. "Women Prophets in the Old Testament." *Priscilla Papers*, The Academy Journal of CBE International (Christians for Biblical Equality.) Spring 2018

Mariottini, Claude. "Women Prophets in the Hebrew Bible." 19 Aug 2013. www.claudemariottini.com

Martin, Shannon. "Who is Rahab?" 29 Aug 2018 www.wisdomwanderings.com/category/strong-biblical-women/

Mathews, Alice. *A Woman God Can Use: Old Testament Women Help You Make Today's Choices*. Discovery House, 2012, Grand Rapids MI (Used by permission of Our Daily Bread Publishing , Box 3566, Grand Rapids, MI 49501. All rights reserved)

Mowczko, Marg. "Abigail: A Bible Beauty with Brains." 8 Mar 21013, https://margmowczko.com/abigail-1-samuel-25/

Papavarnavas, George. "Holy Prophetess Hannah as a Model for Our Lives." 5 Aug 2016 http://orthochristian.com/95949.html

Pope Clement I. *First Epistle to the Corinthians.* 96, (trans. Bart D. Ehrman) *Lost Scriptures: Books That Did Not Make It Into the New Testament.* Oxford University Press, 2013, New York NY

Richards, Sue and Larry. *Every Woman in the Bible.* Thomas Nelson Publishers, 1999, Nashville TN (Used by permission of Thomas Nelson www.thomasnelson.com)

Rosenberg, Roy A. *The Concise Guide to Judaism: History, Practice, Faith.* Penguin Books USA Inc., 1990, New York, NY

Smith-Christopher, Daniel. *The Old Testament: Our Call to Faith and Justice.* 2005. Ave Maria Press Inc., P.O.Box 428, Notre Dame, IN 46556

Tarlow, Peter. "Abigail: A Woman of Strength, Beauty and Valor." 2 Dec 2017, https://www.theeagle.com/brazos_life/abigail-a-woman-of-strength-beauty-and-valor/article

ABOUT THE AUTHOR

Kieran Larkin has taught theology for over 40 years. With a B.A. in Religious Studies from St. Francis College in Brooklyn and an M.A. in Education from NYU, Kieran has taught religion courses in Catholic high school ranging from morality, social justice and world religions to Christology and Old Testament themes. He is the author of "Messengers of God: A Survey of Old Testament Prophets," and has served throughout his adult life as a lector and eucharistic minister. He views the Old Testament prophets—men and women—as especially worthy of adulation for their inspirational and heroic lives and ministries.

ALSO BY KIERAN LARKIN

"Messengers of God: A Survey of Old Testament Prophets"

www.ingramcontent.com/pod-product-compliance
Lightning Source LLC
Chambersburg PA
CBHW030551080526
44585CB00012B/337